POVERTY,
POLITICS, AND
CHANGE

POVERTY, POLITICS, AND CHANGE

DOROTHY BUCKTON JAMES

Herbert H. Lehman College of the City University of New York

PRENTICE-HALL, INC., *Englewood Cliffs, New Jersey*

1972

ISBN: P 0-13-686584-4
C 0-13-686592-5

Library of Congress Catalog Card Number: 70-37390

Printed in the United States of America

10   9   8   7   6   5   4   3

PRENTICE-HALL INTERNATIONAL, INC., *(London)*
PRENTICE-HALL OF AUSTRALIA, PTY. LTD., *(Sydney)*
PRENTICE-HALL OF CANADA, LTD., *(Toronto)*
PRENTICE-HALL OF INDIA PRIVATE LIMITED, *(New Delhi)*
PRENTICE-HALL OF JAPAN, INC., *(Tokyo)*

*To my godchildren, Michael and
Jennifer, in hopes that American values and institutions will have changed toward the
poor before they reach adulthood, and that they
will contribute to further change.*

Preface

"The poor ye have always with you," it seems, because the middle class gets there first. Even though growing concern in scholarly and political circles has produced a myriad of proposals for change, and some substantive governmental programs that purport to be major innovations, the problems posed by persistent, widespread poverty amid affluence continue to plague the nation. American poverty does not yield to the techniques that have been applied or proposed because it is maintained and perpetuated by dominant, pervasive values—individualistic materialism and racism—that are reflected in the nation's social, economic, and political institutions and in the practices and procedures of the professions.

This book attempts to analyze the nature and extent of poverty, the American values that are relevant to it, how they are reflected in policy and in practice, and what impact they have on the poor. It uses these evaluations to assess the most fruitful means of change.

ACKNOWLEDGEMENTS

I shall always be indebted to Professor Lawrence Chamberlain of Columbia University, from whom I learned (albeit slowly) that ideas and institutions interact.

The gracious consideration of several people in reading and commenting on all or part of this manuscript has also been invaluable to me, but my pleasure in acknowledging their help is not intended to implicate them in the errors of the finished product. They include Christian Bay of the University of Alberta, Ernest Collazo, Norman Fainstein of Columbia University, Susan Fainstein of Rutgers University, Gabriel Kolko of the State University of New York at Buffalo, Michael Lipsky of the Massachusetts Institute of Technology, Julie Oliver, Michael Parenti of the University of Vermont, and James Sundquist of The Brookings Institution.

To Ida Fialkin and her able staff—Mary Giacobino, Laura Goldenberg, Linda Gutenstein, Barbara Hoch, and Aida and José Rodriguez—go particular thanks for deciphering my handwriting and typing the drafts of the manuscript.

The debt to my students is particularly heavy because it is they who have helped me to see the questions that should be asked.

Finally, words are inadequate to express my appreciation to Judson James of City College. While my students' questions made this work necessary, his encouragement and intellectual stimulation made it possible.

Contents

THREE

FOUR

FIVE

SIX

SEVEN

THE CHANCES FOR CHANGE 148

INDEX 163

ONE

American Poverty

Poverty is commonly defined in two quite different ways: as a question of *subsistence level*, or as a question of *relative deprivation* compared to the whole society. How poverty is defined matters greatly in approaching the problem of ending poverty, for significantly different public policies spring from the two definitions. Bringing poor families' income up to a minimum subsistence level is an entirely different undertaking from ending the state of relative deprivation in which poor families live. And the choice of definition is related not only to specific public policy-making but also to broader questions of political philosophy.

Even when a definition can be agreed upon, major problems in measuring poverty crop up, and they have serious consequences for public attitudes and policies toward the poor. The difficulties are increased because whichever definition is used, poor people are not homogeneous. Three major categories present themselves—aged poor, rural poor, and urban poor—and each has markedly different needs and political options. Within each of these three groups, moreover, important distinctions appear: the aged poor include people of different races, living in rural and urban settings, alone or as members of families. Rural poor include whites, southern blacks, Mexican Americans, Indians, and migrant farm workers of all races. The urban poor are equally diverse: their ranks include displaced rural whites, blacks, Puerto Rican migrants, Mexican Americans, and Chinese Americans. Each group includes disproportionately large number of families headed by women, and a disproportionate number of young people.

All these factors, and the effects they have on public policy, make

1

it necessary to give careful examination to problems of definition and measurement of poverty. Such examination provides the background for analyzing the causes of poverty and the possibilities for alleviating it.

DEFINING POVERTY

In the popular imagination, "poverty" is being on welfare. The public assumes that the typical poor person is a city-dwelling black woman who is the head of her household of several children because their father (or fathers) have deserted them. She is untrained to earn an adequate living, discriminated against because she is black and female, and in any case unable to get to work because of the small children and the lack of efficient public transportation.

Worse, this stereotypical poor person is thought to have little hope of an improved life-style. Her daughters are likely to follow her pattern, bearing children and going on welfare. They do not fit into the value patterns of the dominant culture in American society. Most damning, they do not seem able to "pull themselves together" and "work for their own salvation."

How much truth is there in the stereotype? Some, but it is not simple to get at. First, we must decide what poverty is; how much deprivation does it take before a person can be called *poor*? How do we decide who those poor people are? How do government data help, and how do they obscure the identifying process? And what poor people are overlooked in the process—and hence passed over when remedies are planned and implemented? How do Eskimos, for example, fit into our notion of the poor and what to do about them? Or old people living on fixed incomes? Or reservation Indian children?

In order to begin answering these questions, we must plunge into a welter of data, not all of it easily categorized or made meaningful. But the weight of the evidence is itself overwhelming: an enormous number of people, mostly white, live at the brink of disaster. Examining their lot may give some insight into the human consequences of their situation, for them and for American society as a whole.

SUBSISTENCE

American political thought has been dominated by the liberal tradition. Before the twentieth century, liberals held that economic questions were not a legitimate subject for public policy. Consequently, little public attempt was made to help poor people. As the liberal view changed on this point, public policy increasingly came to concern itself with how to end or alleviate poverty, which was defined in terms of subsistence level. In formulating and administering public policy toward the poor, therefore, governmental agencies and most analysts have defined poverty in terms of a specific income level based on calculations of the cost of goods necessary for minimal subsistence in the United States.

The "subsistence definition" appears to be both objective and easy to administer, but its apparent simplicity obscures some major problems. The most obvious problem, when we define poverty as an inadequate income for subsistence living, is the meaning of "subsistence." The concept implies that some things are necessary for human existence (meeting minimal standards of nourishment, shelter, and protection from disease), and consequently that goods and services beyond this level are "luxuries." Thus bread is a "necessity," but an automobile is a "luxury." The trouble is that if you live on an Indian reservation in South Dakota, 20 miles from water and 40 miles from a school and the nearest town in which to seek employment, an automobile and the money for fuel and minimal maintenance are necessities on which all others depend.

And the cost of basic necessities varies widely. In urban ghettos, for example, rent is far higher than the rent charged of tenant farmers. Even among urban dwellers, the cost of shelter varies enormously from one part of the country to another; a Harlem resident's rent may be two or three times that of a person living in Cleveland's Hough district or the black ghetto of New Orleans.

The actual amount of money expended on basic necessities such as food may vary greatly. Urban poor people depend almost entirely on buying power—cash and credit—to obtain food; rural poor may supplement income by bartering services, trapping game and fish, and growing, finding, or "liberating" some fresh food.

Finally, differences among the needs of families create problems in applying the subsistence measure; wide variations occur in family size, age, health, location, and general needs.

These problems of defining "subsistence" lie behind the wide variety of arbitrary figures used to establish the poverty level by advocates of this way of defining poverty. One summary of major studies of poverty during the 1960s indicated that:

. . . In a recent study of the Social Security Administration, the costs of an "economy plan" budget for a family of four are estimated at $3195 annually; . . . the study of the Conference for Economic Progress considers "disposable" income below $4000 annually as the poverty line for families and below $2000 for unattached individuals. The Morgan study called those families poor whose disposable income covers less than 90 percent of minimum budgets and who have less than $5000 in assets. According to budgets worked out by the Community Council of Greater New York a family of four (2 adults, 2 children of school age) would need at least $4330. Whatever the basis used, the number of families living below the poverty line is established to fall between 17 percent and 23 percent of the American families.[1]

These estimates of the extent of poverty are modest compared to the estimates of such authors as Michael Harrington or Gunnar Myrdal. Harrington maintained that 40 to 50 million Americans were poor—about a quarter of the population at the time he wrote.[2] To the category "poor" Myrdal added those people suffering from serious deprivation, maintaining that they had to be considered in any broad perspective of economic hardship in the United States.[3] Myrdal found that:

1. Defining *poverty* as an income of $4,000 or less for a multiperson family, or $2,000 for an unattached individual, 38 million Americans, or one-fifth of the nation, lived in poverty. Twelve and a half million of those people (seven percent of the population) lived in utter destitution (defined as half the poverty income or less.)

2. Defining *deprivation* as an income of $4,000 to $6,000 for a multiperson family, or $2,000 to $4,000 for an unattached individual, 39 million more Americans, or another fifth of the population, suffered deprivation.

3. Thus, two-fifths of the population suffered serious economic hardship.

United States Government statistics published shortly after Myrdal wrote suggest that even he underrated the situation. In 1966, for example, the U.S. Department of Labor's "modest but adequate" City Worker's Family Budget called for an average yearly income of $9,191; this income would simply enable a family to obtain those goods and services necessary for a "healthful, self-respecting mode of life, care of children, and participation in community life"—no luxuries included.[4] The incomes of over two-thirds of the nation's families fell below that level. In 1970 the estimate of a moderate budget for a family of four in the New York and northeastern New Jersey area had risen to $11,236 each year. Informal estimates indicated that costs could exceed $11,500 because of a six percent rise in the cost of living from 1969 to 1970.[5]

The human meaning of the official poverty line becomes more stark each year as inflation raises the level of income necessary for "modest" family life. By 1970 the "modest" level for the country as a whole approximated $10,000 annually. Thus, the U.S. government level of $3,700 annual income could produce slow starvation for a family that must purchase essential goods and services during an inflationary spiral which causes severe problems in maintaining a "healthful, self-respecting mode of life" for families who enjoy nearly three times that annual income.

How did $3,000 become the generally accepted "poverty threshold?" This figure was based on standards set by the landmark 1964 report on the extent of poverty in America prepared by the Council of Economic

Advisers, precursor to the "War on Poverty" embodied in the Economic Opportunity Act of 1964. The report, in turn, based its estimates on an earlier study by the Social Security Administration of the income needed to support a nonfarm family of four. This SSA study was based on even earlier estimates of food costs made by the Department of Agriculture.

Analysis of the process by which the $3,000 level was set reveals both the political pressure under which the bureaucracy worked and the slowness with which it responded to change. The 1964 standards were based on those set in 1962, which in turn were based partly on a study of 1955 expenditures; the 1964 figures were then adjusted for political expediency. [The original Social Security Administration standard for a nonfarm family of four:]

. . . provided for a "low cost" budget, permitting the minimum diet consistent with the food preferences of the lowest third of the population and adequate to avoid basic nutritional deficiencies. This budget allowed 28 cents per person per meal, or $3.36 per family per day. On the basis of an Agriculture study made in 1955 showing that 35 percent of the expenditures of low-income families went for food, the size of the total budget was calculated by multiplying the food allowance by three. The resulting budget stood at $3,955. This called for a far higher level of expenditure than welfare agencies were allowing for families receiving public assistance. To meet the administrative need of these bodies, the SSA prepared a second budget. This was an "economy budget" on a deficiency diet designed for temporary emergency use. It allowed 23 cents per person per meal for food or $2.74 per family per day. Multiplied by three, this allowance set the total budget for a nonfarm family of four in 1962 at $3,165. On the basis of this figure, the CEA adopted $3,000 as its family poverty line. In the same way, it arrived at $1,500 as the line for a single individual.[6]

This decision making process tends to refute the supposed objectivity of definitions of poverty based on subsistence level. We are left with the primary reason for its popularity: ease of administrative application. (As we shall see, administrative efficiency, rather than client need, is an underlying theme of much poverty policy.)

Rigid subsistence standards have not, however, been set by the government. They have changed over time. For example, in 1967 the SSA estimated the poverty line for a nonfarm family of four to be $3,410; in 1968 it was $3,553, and in 1969 it had risen to more than $3,700. But bureaucratic change has constantly tended to fall behind need. Moreover, the bureaucracy has responded to a series of pressures that have relegated the needs of the poor to an insignificant position.[7] Political constraints, to be considered more fully in later chapters, have overwhelmingly dominated the standards used by most government agencies to define poverty; thus, during the late 1960s and early 1970s the number of people living in poverty has been seriously underestimated.

Those who favor a subsistence definition of poverty maintain that it functions well when applied to a society in which the increasing gross national product improves the life style of all strata of society. Typical of this attitude was an article entitled "Things Are Getting Better All the Time," which held that:

. . . It simply is not true that any large segment of the American people has been left behind and failed to share in the country's economic progress. . . . if the growth in real income continues, one of its manifestations will be a rise in what is regarded as the standard of poverty so that the poor will continue to be with us. All groups will continue to share in economic progress and the people then labeled poor will have a higher standard of living than many labeled not poor today. How much poverty there is now or will be then depends on the yardstick used to define poverty.[8]

Such a position exhibits great optimism about the speed of change. It enables people to believe that "no one starves in America" and that "real" poverty exists in the "underdeveloped world" but not here. "Real" poverty is indeed more common elsewhere—but by any objective measurement of its attributes (indexes of starvation, malnutrition, or related diseases, for example), poverty is a tragic reality for millions of Americans.

RELATIVE DEPRIVATION

Responding partly to problems of defining an objective standard of subsistence that takes realistic account of the human need involved, many analysts have rejected definitions of poverty based on specific "subsistence" income levels. They have defined poverty in terms relative to the society as a whole. John Kenneth Galbraith maintained that:

. . . People are poverty-stricken when their income, even if adequate for survival, falls markedly behind that of the community. Then they cannot have what the larger community regards as the minimum necessary for decency; and they cannot wholly escape, therefore, the judgment of the larger community that they are indecent. They are degraded for, in the literal sense, they live outside the grades or categories which the community regards as acceptable. . . .[9]

An even broader definition has been suggested by a British writer: "individuals and families whose resources over time, fall seriously short of the resources commanded by the average individual or family in the community in which they live, whether this community is a local, national or international one, are in poverty."[10]

Definitions of poverty in relative terms have thus involved more factors than income adequate for subsistence. They have considered the critical issue to be the shape of income distribution in a society. What these analysts have found is that despite a general rise in the American standard of living since 1947, income distribution has changed very little. The share of the total income received by the lowest fifth of families has remained nearly constant (Table 1.1)[11]:

Table 1.1

CHANGES IN INCOME DISTRIBUTION, 1947–1968

	PERCENTAGE OF AGGREGATE INCOME (BEFORE FEDERAL TAXES) RECEIVED		
FAMILY RANK	*1947*	*1950*	*1968*
Lowest 20 percent	5.0%	4.5%	5.7%
Highest 20 percent	43.0%	42.6%	40.6%
Highest 5 percent	17.2%	17.0%	14.0%

THE DEFINITION AS A GUIDE FOR CHANGE

The "subsistence" definition entails far less extensive change to end poverty. If being poor is a question of not having the power to buy a minimally decent standard of living, by some objective measure, poverty can be ended by the simple device of providing everyone with the income necessary to purchase minimal subsistence. Various means of doing this have been proposed: guaranteed full employment, or guaranteed income for those who cannot be employed (provided by a device like the negative income tax), or a combination of the two.[12] No matter how government provides the income—through direct payments or through employment—the principle is the same: ensure that everyone has the basic necessities for subsistence. Beyond this level, disparities in wealth are perfectly acceptable.

Defining poverty as relative to the standard of living of the whole society means that poverty could be ended only by thoroughly restructuring the distribution of wealth in the United States. Such a redistribution would entail major changes in the social, economic, and political orders. But the values that dominate American life make such changes impossible short of violent revolution—and adherence to these values runs so broad and deep that such revolution is highly unlikely to happen. Indeed, these values are so strong that they make it extremely difficult to accomplish even the modest changes required to provide a minimium subsistence for every American.

The subsistence standard established by the U.S. government must be the one chosen for use here. It has been selected only because most available measurements of poverty depend upon it, and it thus becomes the only basis on which a wide body of data can be discussed. Bear in mind, however, that these data tend to seriously underrepresent the number of people who cannot provide themselves with essential food, shelter, and services, much less a degree of human self-respect.

MEASURING POVERTY

Beyond defining poverty, major problems obstruct those who would measure its extent and diversity. Many poor people are invisible when it comes to data collection. The process of measuring poverty involves substantial errors that underestimate its extent by millions of people, especially among non-whites, and limit the degree to which its diversity can be assessed. These errors stem from public apathy and the problems inherent in collecting data from a poor population.

PUBLIC APATHY

A society's values are clearly mirrored in the data its official institutions choose to collect and interpret, because the categories that are investigated or omitted reflect society's major concerns. The questions asked by the U.S. Bureau of the Census show the degree to which American society emphasizes materialistic, consumer-oriented, racist values. For example, while millions of poor people are statistically invisible, accurate accounting is made of the nation's indoor toilets and television sets.

Even the naming of categories has import: mainstream America perceives its world in terms of its own racial category, "white," lumping all other races together under an amorphous "nonwhite"—that is, "not like us."* The statistics derived from this process of data-gathering mask enormous diversity among the nonwhite population, and these diverse traits are related to public policy. For example, in the late 1960s the U.S. government's determination of life expectancy rates set the average life of white males at 67.6 years and white females at 74.7 years; nonwhite males averaged 60.7 years and nonwhite females 67.4 years. Had the category "nonwhite" been broken down into its components, startling differences would have appeared—for example, among Orientals, blacks, and Indians. The average life expectancy of American Indians stood at an astonishingly low 42 years; within this category, Eskimo life expectancy was only 35 years.[13] These low life expectancy rates apply to just those Americans who depend most heavily on government policy—and the government's own statistical analysis obscures these rates. Similarly,

---

*The "nonwhite" population is predominantly black, but it includes substantial numbers of other minorities. The breakdown within the total U.S. population is: Blacks, 12%; Mexican Americans, 2%; Puerto Ricans, .5%; Orientals, .5%; Amercan Indians, .25%.

it is difficult to obtain an accurate measure of poverty among the aged because U.S. government statistics group poor people by family status. It is possible to judge the poverty of families headed by people over 65 but not of unattached individuals over 65. Unattached individuals of all ages are lumped together in one category in government compilations of income level. One might assume that a large proportion of the aged poor live alone, and that these aged have the lowest income levels of all; but without adequate data the question remains unanswered.

ADMINISTERING SURVEYS

Even if the right questions were to be asked, measuring poverty precisely would still present serious problems. How does one get a conscientious survey out of field workers who often must administer questionnaires in areas that are physically dangerous (broken stairs, falling plaster, rats, threat of physical assault). How can one solve the problem that the poor do not trust government officials? Mutual fear and hostility have always led to underenumeration of the poor, particularly the "nonwhite" poor. The U.S. Bureau of the Census estimates that its own 1960 Census omitted counting as many as 14 percent of all black males (compared to two percent of all white males).[14] Thus, whatever the cause, the net result of persistent significant errors in measurement is invisibility for a large proportion of the American poor.

WHO ARE THE POOR?

No matter how poverty is defined or measured, certain categories tend to appear disproportionately among the poor, and each has its particular needs and political options. At this point it may be useful to define the nature and diversity of their need.   V

The vast majority of the poor in each category are white. In fact, whites constitute two-thirds of Americans below the government-defined poverty threshold. The "nonwhite" groups are disproportionately represented among the poor because they make up a far greater proportion of the poor population than of the American population as a whole (see Figure 1–1).

THE AGED POOR

Poverty is most prevalent among people 65 or older. In 1968 a quarter of these older Americans were classified as poor. They made up 18 percent of the *total* poor.[15] About half were living alone,[16] but families (two or more people) headed by a person 65 or older constituted a full third of all poor *families*. Of these families a majority lived in utter destitution, supported on less than $1,000 a year. Their position was suc-

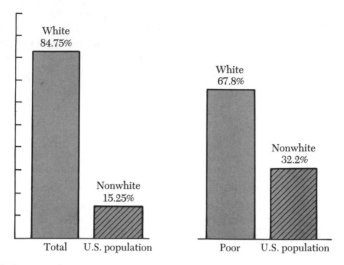

Figure 1-1

cinctly summarized in Sargent Shriver's testimony before the Senate
Committee on Labor and Public Welfare:

> Many of the aged are ending in poverty because they began in poverty. Their
> income throughout their working lives was never sufficient to provide that
> margin of savings which affords independence and dignity after retirement.
>   The majority of all the aged are covered by social security. But nearly
> two-thirds of the poorest—those living alone and earning less than $1,000 a
> year—are not covered by social security.
>   The great medical advances which continually discover new ways to pro-
> long life have assured a steady growth in the number of aged persons in our
> society, and accordingly a growth in the problems of the aged. During the last
> 15 years the number of aged heads of families increased 37 percent. It is esti-
> mated that by 1980 there will be 9 million persons over 75 in this country and
> if the present pattern is allowed to continue, many millions of them will be
> living in stark poverty.[17]

Thus, the problem of the aged poor is growing. These older poor
people are likely to remain unemployable because of ill health and because employment practices discriminate heavily on grounds of age,[18]
sex (two-thirds of all the elderly poor are female), and race (47 percent
of nonwhite aged are poor, compared to 25 percent of the white aged).[19]
Of all poor people, the aged are the least likely to rise above poverty
by their own efforts.

Not all the aged poor have experienced a lifetime of poverty. A
substantial group are people who belonged to the working class or the

middle class during their working years, but whose retirement incomes were inadequate for subsistence. Included are such people as those whose savings have been eaten up by heavy medical expenses, or widows whose husbands were unable to provide adequately for them.

THE RURAL POOR

The rural poor include people who live on the land they own and people who are tenant farmers, hired hands, or migrant farm workers. Racially and ethnically quite diverse, they are predominantly white but include a substantial proportion of southern blacks, Mexican Americans in the South and West, Indians on reservation land, and Puerto Rican migrants in the East.

The proportion of America's poor living in rural areas has steadily declined over the past decade. Between 1959 and 1968 poor persons living on farms diminished from eight million to 2.3 million, which reduced the percentage of poor people in the total farm population from 50.5 percent to 22.7 percent.[20] This trend seems likely to continue, but the reduction in rural poor indicates not an improvement in the lot of the rural population, but rather the reverse. To many residents of rural America, poverty has been such an inescapable fact of life that the problem has simply been moved to urban areas, through major migration by all the races that make up the rural poor. Moreover, the mobile have tended to be younger, more ambitious, or better educated; thus, the rural poor who remained in the country have been those least able to better their condition.[21]

About a quarter of all persons living on farms in America have been found to be poor, compared to 18 percent of those residing in nonfarm areas.[22] The poverty study that provided a background for the Economic Opportunity Act of 1964 found extreme differences, based on race, in the extent of this rural poverty. More than 80 percent of "nonwhite" farmers were found to be poor.[23] When the components of that "nonwhite" category are considered, a stark picture emerges. Of these minorities the Indian has suffered the greatest deprivation. He lives in the poorest housing (90 percent of it below minimal standards of safety, health, and decency), is the least educated (50 percent literate), has the least secure employment (unemployment rate seven times the national average), and, because of malnutrition and disease, "enjoys" the shortest life span (42 years).[24] In 1969 the average *family* income for all American Indians was $1,500.[25]

Three and a half million Mexican Americans, concentrated in the Southwest, make up the nation's second largest minority, nearly a quarter of whom live in rural areas. Two-thirds of Mexican-American families lived on less than $3,000 a year during the last decade,[26] and these families were heavily concentrated in rural areas. Ten percent of all black families, or about half a million families, lived in rural poverty, primarily in the South.[27]

Although some whites are included among migrant farm workers, this category comprises mainly blacks, Mexican Americans in the West, and Puerto Ricans in the East. These rural poor have suffered extreme deprivation. One recent study found that two-thirds of all migrant workers earned less than $1,000 each year from both farm and nonfarm work.[28] Actually, income figures for migrants have been deceptive because a migrant handles little cash: "By payday he owes most of it to the crew leader of the store."[29] Long periods without work are typical, and about 40 percent experience some form of involuntary unemployment. Family earnings of migrants provided an even bleaker picture. A Senate committee found that families including three or more farm workers earned an average *total* annual income of $1,432.[30] Extreme discrepancies in migrant income also showed up in different regions of the country. Whereas California migrants often reported incomes as high as $2,000 annually, in the East annual incomes of $500 and $600 were often reported.[31]

This is a depressing picture for a nation whose school children regularly sing the praises of America's "amber fields of grain" and "fruited plain," though it is no more unreal than the song's assertion that "her alabaster cities gleam undimmed by human tears."

THE URBAN POOR

In 1968 about half of America's poor people lived in metropolitan areas comprising central cities surrounded by rings of suburbs. Of these metropolitan poor, two-thirds inhabited the central cities and a third lived in the suburbs. Over 90 percent of the suburban poor were white. (Advance interpretations of the 1970 Census data indicate a significant shift of "nonwhite" population to the suburbs). Poverty in the suburbs has had little study, and the suburban poor have been relatively invisible. Thus, their distinctive characteristics and particular needs cannot be considered in formulating public policy until more research has been done.

In central cities the white share of the poor population dropped to 57 percent.[32] Many of these people were displaced rural whites (e.g., "Okie" settlers in California cities, and the "hillbilly" ghetto in Chicago). Forty-three percent of the poor in central cities were black. Almost all American cities had concentrations of blacks living in the core; Puerto Ricans were living mainly in the Northeast, with three-fourths of the

Puerto Rican population on the U.S. mainland residing in New York City. Mexican Americans clustered in the Southwest, and Chinese inhabited enclaves in San Francisco, New York, and Boston.

Of these groups, by far the largest was black. A third of all blacks lived in the 12 largest U.S. cities, often in heavy concentrations. The population of Washington, D.C., was nearly two-thirds black. Newark, N.J., was over half black; Baltimore and St. Louis, over a third black; and Chicago and Philadelphia, nearly a third black.[33] More typical of national patterns was New York City, where blacks and Puerto Ricans constituted a fifth of the central-city population. To these figures must be added the substantial black population living in smaller cities, particularly in the South. Thus, the majority of blacks in America lived in central cities, where the incidence of poverty was high. Considered in terms of family units, about half a million families, or ten percent of all black families in America, lived in urban poverty.[34]

About a million Puerto Ricans have come to live on the mainland in the last several decades, settling heavily in the Northeast. Three-quarters of them live in New York City, primarily in the core-city poverty areas of central and east Harlem, the south Bronx, and Bedford-Stuyvesant in Brooklyn. In 1969 a federal study of New York City's Puerto Rican population found that they were the poorest group in the city.[35] They had the greatest trouble getting and keeping jobs, even if they were physically able to look for them; many were found to have physical or mental disabilities that incapacitated them for work. Even those who found jobs frequently had only part-time work or were forced in full-time jobs to work for less than the federal minimum wage. For example, of 157,000 working Puerto Rican men and women, 10.7 percent earned less than the federal minimum. In length of unemployment Puerto Ricans suffered more than any other group: 26.2 percent were unemployed for 5 to 14 weeks and 27.4 percent were unemployed for 15 weeks or more, which equaled the worst rate of unemployment America had experienced, in 1933, at the bottom of the Great Depression. A 1970 report by the Bureau of Labor Statistics indicated that the unemployment rate for Puerto Rican males 25 to 54 years old was nearly twice that of black males in this age range, and almost five times the rate for the nation's labor force as a whole.[36]

During the 1950s and early 1960s, the Mexican-American population shifted heavily toward urban areas of the Southwest. More than three-quarters of this population lived in urban areas in five Southwestern states: California, Nevada, Arizona, New Mexico, and Texas,[37] with major concentrations in Texas and California. Two-thirds of all these families lived at or below the poverty threshold during the 1960s.

The Chinese-American poor are more difficult to discuss than other groups of urban poor because even less comprehensive study has been devoted to them. Studies available from the three cities where most Chinese Americans live (San Francisco, New York, and Boston) are indicative of this group's poverty. A 1969 study in New York City found that although employment rates were high, hours were extremely long and pay very low. Over 15 percent of employed Chinese Americans worked 49 to 59 hours per week, and another 20 percent worked 60 hours or more a week.[38] They were employed chiefly in restaurants, laundries, cloth or garment factories, and as unskilled labor. Compared to the median income for all families in the metropolitan area, or even to the median income for black families in the area, residents of Chinatown were at a severe disadvantage[39] (Table 1.2). To make these figures even more striking, in over 70 percent of these families, women were working as well as men. Thus, this low family income usually represented full-time work of at least two adults.[40] A similar picture came from Boston, where the Chinese ghetto had the lowest median family income in the city.[41]

DEPENDENT CHILDREN

The disproportionately large number of young people living in poverty is a particular problem of the urban poor, though the rural poor share it, too. Of a 1967 total population of 26.1 million poor persons, 10.7 million were children under 18.[42] Thus, 41 percent of the total poor population was under 18 years old.

The poverty of children is a particular problem for minority groups because these groups contain a higher proportion of children than does the white population. For example, the median age for blacks in 1969 was 21; thus, a substantial proportion of the entire black population were minors.[43] Similarly, almost half of the Puerto Rican population on the U.S. mainland was under 21, with 84 percent of those Puerto Ricans born in the United States of Puerto Rican parents being under 14.[44] The median age of Mexican Americans was just over 19 years.[45]

Poor children were disproportionately concentrated in "nonwhite" poor families (see Table 1.3).[46] The poverty of children is associated

Table 1.2

1966 MEDIAN INCOME IN NORTH CENTRAL
METROPOLITAN AREAS

White families	$9,184
Black families	6,018
Families in Chinatown	4,500

Table 1.3

PERCENTAGE OF CHILDREN UNDER 18 LIVING IN POVERTY, 1968

AREA	ALL RACES	WHITES	NONWHITES
	(%)	*(%)*	*(%)*
United States	15.3	10.7	41.6
Metropolitan Areas	12.2	7.9	33.5
Central cities	17.6	11.0	33.5
Suburbs	8.2	6.3	33.4
Nonmetropolitan Areas	20.9	15.4	58.4
Nonfarm	19.3	14.2	55.1
Farm	33.6	25.4	79.7

with two factors: the presence or absence of a father and the size of the family. In 1968 the poverty rate for children who were living in families headed by women was 53.6 percent. This was eight times as high as the rate (6.5 percent) for children living in families with male heads.[47] The direct correlation between family size and poverty among children may be seen in Table 1.4.[48]

THE STATUS OF WOMEN

Families headed by women are disproportionately represented among all three categories of the poor: the aged, rural, and urban poor. Among whites, 36 percent of households headed by women with dependent children were poor in 1968, whereas almost two-thirds (62 percent) of all nonwhite families headed by women were poor. These woman-headed households contained seven million poor persons.[49]

Underlying those statistics are some important facts of social or-

Table 1.4

IMPOVERISHED CHIDREN UNDER 18 BY SIZE OF FAMILY, 1968

NUMBER OF CHILDREN IN FAMILY	PERCENTAGE OF FAMILIES IN POVERTY		
	White	*Nonwhite*	*All*
None	7.3	16.8	8.0
One	6.3	20.9	7.9
Two	6.1	26.8	8.1
Three	9.1	34.0	11.8
Four	11.6	41.9	16.0
Five	21.5	50.2	27.5
Six or more	23.3	58.4	34.4

ganization: women are "programmed" to be unable to earn a living wage; widespread discrimination against women is practiced in hiring and salary policies; and most communities lack the facilities that would enable mothers to work if they could overcome the first two handicaps.[50]

Women are programmed in the sense that marriage and child-bearing are the primary career goals to which the socializing institutions (family, church, school) direct them. (Boys, on the other hand, are offered a wide range of career options.) Consequently, girls tend to be shunted into training for low-paying "temporary" jobs: typists, secretaries, clerks, waitresses, sales personnel. Even the professions into which the more able or ambitious have been channeled (elementary and secondary school teaching, nursing, library science, social work) have had very low wage scales *because* they were staffed by women. Significantly, as men more often entered teaching and library science, the wage scales rose markedly, but men were then preferred over women in hiring practices. In professional work, women have traditionally been "last hired, first fired." This type of "programming" is significant in the sense that it seriously hinders most women from earning a wage large enough to support a family should the husband's income cease through death, illness, divorce, or desertion.

Even if a woman has special skills or training, she is discriminated against in hiring practices and wage scales. Employers prefer men on the mythical grounds that women lose more days of work than men, that their turnover rate is far higher, and that they inherently lack the intellectual attributes necessary to professional work. All these assumptions are false:

1. *Loss of working time.* The U.S. Department of Labor reports that "the worktime lost by persons 17 years of age and over because of illness or injury averaged 5.3 days for women and 5.4 days for men over the same period."[51]

2. *Turnover rate.* The same report indicates that turnover rate is influenced more by the skill level and stability level of the job, age of the worker, and the worker's length of service with the employer than by sex differences. The turnover rate for male and female workers was similar.[52] Actually, employers tend seriously to underestimate the turnover of males, exclusive of the draft.[53]

3. *Intellectual and motivational incapacity for professional work.* Those women who do overcome the barriers to admission to medical or law school have been found consistently to have completed their training at the top of their classes.[54] Moreover, the percentage of men and women completing professional school training is about the same, 84 percent.

Discrimination in wage scales is indicated in a number of studies by the Women's Bureau of the United States Department of Labor. Women Ph.D.s, for example, even after they have overcome all the barriers of socialization, gotten admitted to graduate school, and gotten a job, earn an average annual income that is $2,000 less than the average for male Ph.D.s. And the median wage of all American women who worked full-time, year-round in 1968 was only 58 percent of men's.[55]

Retraining is another problem that a woman who has been away from work raising a family must face, if circumstances deprive the family of its male breadwinner. After an absence of several years, a woman probably would need to retrain for her former job but such courses are not readily available, and companies tend to prefer to train young workers rather than retrain older ones. The older the woman is, the more severe are the barriers to her reemployment. The final factor that underlies the poverty of families headed by women is the fact that most communities lack both day-care centers and adequate public transportation that would free a mother to work.

The largest single category of the poor is dependent children, and this category is growing rapidly. They are poor for one major reason: they live in families headed by women. Consequently, the inability of women to earn a living wage in American society vastly increases the proportion of poverty in the nation. An argument made by many is that if women earned a living wage, men would be put out of work, which would merely redistribute poverty. This argument is economically unsound because raising the wage level creates more disposable income, which in turn creates more jobs. Keeping people in a state of poverty is economically wasteful for the entire society.

CONCLUSION

Poor people in America share many common needs, but their varied characteristics call for specialized programs as well. Before considering what *should* be done, we need to consider what has and has not been done in America, and why. The following chapters will attempt to explain what has and has not been done in terms of dominant American values, and the social, economic and political organizations that both reflect and reinforce those values.

Notes

1. HANNA H. MEISSNER, ed., *Poverty in the Affluent Society* (New York: Harper & Row, 1966), pp. 40–41.
2. MICHAEL HARRINGTON, *The Other America* (New York: Macmillan, 1962).
3. GUNNAR MYRDAL, *Challenge to Affluence* (New York: Vintage Books, 1965).
4. MAURICE ZEITLIN, ed., *American Society, Inc.* (Chicago: Markham, 1970), p. 152.
5. *The New York Times*, January 5, 1970, 1:1.
6. CLAIR WILCOX, *Toward Social Welfare* (Homewood, Ill.: Richard D. Irwin, 1969), pp. 26–27.
7. S. M. MILLER and PAMELA A. ROBY, *The Future of Inequality* (New York: Basic Books, 1970), p. 35.
8. ROSE D. FRIEDMAN, "Things are Getting Better All the Time," in Herman P. Miller, ed., *Poverty American Style* (Belmont, Calif.: Wadsworth, 1968), p. 38.
9. JOHN KENNETH GALBRAITH, *The Affluent Society* (New York: New American Library, 1958), p. 251.
10. PETER TOWNSEND, "The Meaning of Poverty," *British Journal of Sociology*, 13 (1962), 225.
11. ANTHONY DOWNS, *Who Are the Urban Poor?* (New York: Committee for Economic Development, 1970), p. 10.
12. LEON H. KEYSERLING in *Dialogue on Poverty* (Indianapolis and New York: Bobbs and Merrill, 1967), pp. 91–104.
13. "The American Indian, Dispossessed and Abandoned," in ROBERT E. WILL and HAROLD G. VATTER, eds., *Poverty in Affluence* (New York: Harcourt, Brace & World, 1965), p. 163.
14. Reported in *The New York Times Magazine*, August 2, 1970, p. 28.
15. A statement on national policy by the Research and Policy Committee of the Committee for Economic Development, "Improving the Public Welfare System," April 1970, p. 26; Hereafter cited as "C.E.D. statement."
16. *Ibid.*, p. 28.
17. SARGENT SHRIVER, "The Aged," in WILL and VATTER, *Poverty in Affluence*, pp. 178–179.

18. MICHAEL J. BRENNAN, PHILIP TAFT, and MARK B. SCHUPACK, The Economics of Age (New York: W. W. Norton, 1967).

19. C.E.D. statement, p. 28.

20. Ibid., p. 23.

21. For discussion of this migration pattern by Appalachian whites see HARRY CAUDILL, Night Comes to the Cumberlands (Boston: Little Brown, 1963); WILLIAM J. PAGE, JR., and EARL E. HUYEK, "Appalachia: Realities of Deprivation," in BEN B. SELIGMAN, ed., Poverty as a Public Issue (New York: Free Press, 1965), pp. 152–176.

22. Table from Social Security Bulletin, January 1965, reprinted in HERMAN P. MILLER, ed., Poverty American Style (Belmont, Calif.: Wadsworth, 1968), p. 116.

23. Poverty in the United States, Report to the House Committee on Education and Labor (Washington, D. C.: U.S. Government Printing Office, 1964).

24. WILCOX, Toward Social Welfare, p. 52.

25. Association on American Indian Affairs, Newsletter, Fall 1969.

26. DONALD N. BARRETT, "Demographic Characteristics," in JULIAN SAMORA, ed., La Raza: Forgotten Americans (Notre Dame, Ind.: University of Notre Dame Press, 1966).

27. Statistics compiled from the Bureau of Labor Statistics and Bureau of the Census by JOHN F. KAIN, ed., Race and Poverty: The Economics of Discrimination (Englewood Cliffs, N. J.: Prentice-Hall, 1969), p. 37.

28. LENORE EPSTEIN, "Migratory Farm Workers" in WILL and VATTER, Poverty in Affluence, pp. 112–113.

29. TRUMAN MOORE, The Slaves We Rent (New York: Random House, 1965), p. 139.

30. Senate Committee on Labor and Public Welfare, Subcommittee on Migratory Labor, "The Migratory Farm Labor Problem in the United States" (Washington D.C.: U.S. Government Printing Office, 1965), p. 1.

31. MOORE, The Slaves We Rent, p. 139.

32. C.E.D. statement, p. 23.

33. WILCOX, Toward Social Welfare, p. 54.

34. KAIN, Race and Poverty, p. 37.

35. Reported in The New York Times, November 17, 1969, 32:1.

36. The New York Times, July 10, 1970, 36:4.

37. DONALD N. BARRETT in SAMORA, La Raza: Forgotten Americans, pp. 163, 194–196.

38. Chinatown Report, 1969 (New York: Chinatown Study Group, 1970), p. 18. This report is available at the Chatham Square Branch of the New York Public Library.

39. Ibid., p. 56.

40. Ibid., p. 57.

41. The Urban Reporter, January 20, 1971, p. 4.

42. U.S. Bureau of the Census, Statistical Abstracts of the United States: 1969 (90th edition; Washington, D.C.: U.S. Government Printing Office, 1969), Table 484, p. 328.

43. *Newsweek*, 73 (June 30, 1969), p. 18.

44. Joseph Monserrat, "Puetro Rican Migration," speech before Symposium on Puerto Rico in the year 2,000, reprinted by the *Howard University Law Journal* (Washington, D.C., 1968).

45. Donald N. Barrett in Samora, *La Raza: Forgotten Americans*, p. 170.

46. Downs, *Who Are the Urban Poor?*, p. 25.

47. *Ibid.*, p. 26.

48. *Ibid.*, p. 27. See also C.E.D. statement, p. 28.

49. C.E.D. statement, pp. 28–29.

50. For a more thorough discussion of these factors see Kirsten Amundsen, *The Silenced Majority: Women and American Democracy* (Englewood Cliffs, N. J.: Prentice-Hall, 1971), chaps. 2 and 3.

51. Women's Bureau, United States Department of Labor, *1969 Handbook on Women Workers* (Washington, D.C.: U.S. Government Printing Office, 1969), p. 80.

52. *Ibid.*, p. 76.

53. Warren Farrell, "The Resocialization of Men's Attitudes Toward Women's Role in Society," paper presented to the American Political Science Association Annual Meeting (Los Angeles, September 9, 1970), p. 6.

54. *Ibid.*, p. 7.

55. Address by Elizabeth Duncan Koontz, director of the Women's Bureau, United States Department of Labor, "American Women at the Crossroads," Keynote Address at the 50th Anniversary Conference of the Women's Bureau (Washington, D.C., June 12, 1970).

TWO

American Values that Maintain
and Perpetuate Poverty

Having made a start at identifying and characterizing various groups of poor people, we may well consider how society at large regards them. What values predominate that tend to perpetuate poverty? How does American society create its poor and then hold them in that state?

Most important, within America's context of values, what are the chances for change?

American history is marked by a pattern of continuous protest by individuals and groups seeking alternatives to prevailing values. Nevertheless, two values have consistently dominated American thought and public policy from the seventeenth century to the present: ethnocentrism, and liberalism. Individualism and materialism are the twin pillars of liberal thought. These values are reflected in all aspects of public policy, including policy affecting the poor. Their strength has severely limited the degree to which Americans have been willing even to consider poverty a legitimate target of public policy, and has narrowly restricted the alternative policies that have been acceptable to the electorate.

Beyond public policy-making these values have been reflected in the practices of those professions that transmit society's norms to the poor. The brief analysis (Chapter Four) of practices and procedures in education, law, medicine, and social work gives a view of the socialization process through which the poor have developed their own self-image in American society. It substantiates the position that the nation's value system has materially contributed to creating and perpetuating poverty in America.

MATERIALISTIC INDIVIDUALISM AND ETHNOCENTRISM

Although the basic traditions of modern Western political thought provide several alternatives, analysis of American thought shows that all but one philosophy has been largely ignored or rejected. The United States has been dominated by the liberal tradition. Because public policy toward the poor has reflected liberalism's emphasis on materialistic individualism, that policy has helped to create and perpetuate poverty.

LIBERALISM, CONSERVATISM, AND SOCIALISM

During the past 250 years Western political thought has been dominated by three traditions: liberalism, conservatism, and socialism. The ways in which these three traditions approach the relationship between the individual and society, and the function of government, may give some insight into American values as they relate to the poor.

Liberalism began as a revolt against authoritarian government. It aimed at liberation, seeking to free people from the restraints of traditional hierarchical authority. Despite differences that developed between liberals on the question of the functions that it was legitimate for government to perform, all liberals focused on the needs of *individuals*, relegating the needs of the state, church, or society to a secondary, or even an irrelevant position. Thus liberalism stressed individual freedom and equality, asserting that individuals had an *inherent* right to seek *private* ends, which meant that individuals must be free to have and use private property.

Initially, liberal thought emphasized unrestricted use of private property. Developments in liberal thought by the twentieth century led to acceptance of the necessity for partial restriction of an individual's use of his private property to the degree that it interfered with other individuals' ability to develop their mental and moral resources.[1] However, even those liberals who accepted the need for some government regulation of private property expected that this would not pose a major problem because they *assumed* that men were both capable of rational choice and shared similar needs and goals that could be the basis of public policy.

Through much of its history, as a result of its stress on individualistic materialism, liberalism held a negative view of government's appropriate function. Thus, for most liberals prior to the twentieth century, government's only legitimate function was to protect individuals in the full enjoyment of their life, liberty, and property, and perhaps to provide those services necessary for protection that individuals could not themselves provide, such as lighthouses or post roads. As a result of this dual stress on individual freedom to pursue private ends and individual equality, liberalism supported capitalism ("free enterprise") as the most appropriate form of economic organization and democracy ("majority rule") as the only acceptable form of political organization. In stressing the individual's right to indulge in economic competition without governmental interference, it denied that poverty could be a legitimate subject for public policy. Poor people were seen as no different from anyone else: individuals whose position in society would be determined by their ability, and who should be protected from government interference with their right to compete economically with others. Their status reflected their ability in this competition.

Liberalism has passed through three phases; each has stressed human freedom and equality, but each has justified its position differently. Early liberals justified human freedom by means of a concept of a natural order; later liberals justified it on the utilitarian ground that it would bring the greatest happiness to the greatest number; and the third group justified it on the basis of the organic relationship between individual and social growth. Initially, liberal writers who believed in a natural order, such as John Locke, proposed a three part argument to justify individual freedom and equality:[2]

1. God has established laws to order all creation, and the National Law that He has set for man holds that each man (equality) should be free in his life, liberty, and property (i.e., he may pursue private ends).

2. Man can know these laws because God has given him reason.

3. Therefore, man is capable of establishing government to enforce these laws (i.e., the sole legitimate purpose of government is protection of individual life, liberty, and property). Thus, governments are created by contract among free and equal individuals.

Such a view entailed two key assumptions that later political theorists were not prepared to accept. First, it assumed that God had set a natural order for His creation. Second, it assumed that man was capable of knowing that order. A generation after Locke, David Hume mounted a major assault on these assumptions.[3] He maintained that whether God had established rules for His creation was irrelevant because man could never know them. He held that man could know only primary (sensory) impressions or secondary ones (passions) and ideas that were less vivid copies of them. Human reason could not add anything to these impressions. Reason operated merely to analyze and generalize on the basis of sensory impressions (pleasure or pain) and passions. Since man could not experience God or Natural Law, he could not "know" them. Man merely imagined such abstractions, which explained why human practice varied so much in following what Locke asserted to be self-evident natural laws.

Hume demolished the idea that government originated in a social contract by demonstrating that throughout human history almost all governments had originally been founded on usurpation, conquest, or both. These governments were obeyed merely from habit, not consent; that is, government became so familiar that most men never question its origin or cause. For Hume, governments originated not in contract but in human need. Through trial and error individuals learned that their pleasure was maximized and pain minimized if they had protection of their life, liberty, and property. They also learned that individuals were shortsighted; it was useful to establish a means of restraining immediate individual impulses in order to ensure the greatest happiness of the greatest number of people. Government enabled individuals to act in their own long-term self-interest by permitting them to resist immediate temptations through a system of rewards and punishments. Government did not make men less shortsighted; rather, it made the immediate interest of some men (the governors) to enforce the rules. Thus, Hume maintained that utility dictated that men follow government, but custom dictated which form they would follow. The form developed gradually by convention, and for the masses it happened unconsciously, not through a rational social contract.

This doctrine was labeled "utilitarianism" because it justified government on the ground of its being useful to man. The doctrine was based in egoistic individualism, assuming that pleasure alone was "good" and that the equal pleasures of any two or more men were equally good, that men would strive to maximize their pleasure, and that government's only legitimate function was to ensure the greatest happiness for the greatest number.

This philosophy was the basis for Adam Smith's justification of *laissez-faire* economics.[4] Smith believed that a natural harmony existed in the economic order; he expressed this harmony through the image of an "invisible hand." If left unrestrained, natural harmony would work for the greatest good of the greatest number. Consequently, government should not interfere in the economy because any such interference would destroy the balance maintained by the "invisible hand."

Locke, Hume, and Smith differed about the nature of knowledge and the origin of government, but these proponents of natural law and utilitarianism agreed in focusing on individual liberty and equality, and in limiting the role of government to protection of life, liberty, and property. Implicit in their view was the denial that poverty could be a legitimate subject of public policy—and this denial brought liberalism under attack from both conservatives and socialists. Responding to the charge that the denial was unrealistic, liberalism developed a third phase, "organic liberalism," which will be explained more fully after consideration of the issues raised by conservatism and socialism.

Conservatism: Conservatives and socialists agreed on at least one thing: the social order was superior to privately determined individual rights. They conceived of individuals as part of an organic whole, creations of their society. The conservative tradition emphasized inherent human inequality. It approached the organization of a society with religious reverence, considering it the product of the slow, invisible working of history. Conservatives found it impossible to accept the liberal faith that constitutions were made by individuals assembled in parliaments and conventions. Edmund Burke wrote that the tradition of the society's constitution ought to be the object of a reverence akin to religion, because it formed the repository of a collective intelligence and civilization.[5] He held that natural social equality was fictitious. Rather, the natural differences of rank that existed in any political system arose from a natural division of labor. Burke maintained that the natural aristocracy should rule: men of ability, birth, and wealth should lead. Like contemporary liberals, but for entirely different reasons, conservatives of the era agreed that poverty was not a legitimate subject for public policy. The state could do nothing to aid its poor, nor should it try.

European conservatives went considerably further than Burke in emphasizing the mystical qualities of the state that deserved man's reverence. Joseph de Maistre maintained that government was necessitated by man's original sin and that government's function was to force the correct prejudices upon man, through mastery and terror, until he behaved well enough to maintain social order.[6] Louis de Bonald agreed that religion was the only firm basis for social organization.[7] Johann Fichte maintained that the state had a mystical quality, it was an organic whole that required the devotion and sacrifice of individuals.[8]

Socialism shared the idea that the social order was superior to privately determined individual rights but placed no such emphasis on tradition, religion, or inherent human inequality. Rather, the socialist philosophy that developed before Karl Marx emphasized the social element in human relationships in contrast to the liberal stress on individualism that prevailed in England and France at the end of the eighteenth century and beginning of the nineteenth.[9] Pre-Marxian socialists were in substantial agreement on some major considerations:

1. Men should promote the *general* well-being.
2. The general well-being was incompatible with any social order based on a competitive struggle for the means of livelihood (rejection of laissez faire).
3. Economic forces took precedence over political ones. (Socialists

distrusted government, "politics," and politicians, preferring a system in which control of social affairs would lie with the "producers.")

Karl Marx labeled these socialists "utopian," and thought them politically naive, but he shared and developed their attribution of social life and development entirely to the economic factor. Consequently, he shared their belief in the necessity for subordination of individual interests to the general good.[10] Thus, socialist thought maintained that poverty was not the result of individual failure but of economic and social forces, and that these forces were appropriate subjects for public policy. The state could act to eradicate poverty, and it should do so.

As socialism developed, it increasingly emphasized the necessity for overall, comprehensive planning of public policy for the general good. Consequently, it was ambivalent on the question of human equality. It anticipated a classless society of equal humans as the ultimate expression of the socialist ideal; but Leninist and Stalinist writers assumed that during the transitional period (unspecified duration) an elite (technical experts, or "the vanguard," or "the party") would plan for the masses.

Organic liberalism developed as an attempt to respond to both the criticism raised by conservatives and socialists that individuals were created by their society, and to the severe problems that arose in England and America where *laissez faire* had become public policy. Liberal support for *laissez faire* economics had been intended only as a means to advance the greatest good of the greatest number but it had become a bulwark of reaction and privilege. This discrepancy between theory and practice resulted from an erroneous assumption in the theory. To have a free enterprise system individuals must be able to bargain freely, but in reality bargaining power between major experienced industrialists and their unorganized workers meant that neither individual freedom nor equality were enjoyed.

T. H. Green[11] faced this problem head on: He never discarded the liberal adherence to individual freedom and equality and the inherent right of individuals to seek private ends, but he took an *organic* view of society. While he would agree with earlier liberals that society is nothing other than the lives of individuals as they act upon one another, he added that their lives would be quite different if separated from society. In fact part of their lives would be nonexistent.

Therefore, Green believed that earlier liberal thinking had been too narrow. In seeking to free the individual it had focused solely on negative freedom, freedom *from* governmental restraint. But even when a person is freed from governmental restraint, he still may be unable to develop his moral and intellectual potential because social or economic factors may repress him. For example, even if neither law nor governmental regulation limited the freedom of a black man in Sunflower County, Mississippi, social patterns of racial discrimination would limit him. Similarly, a starving man, or a man mutilated in an accident in an unsafe factory, or incapacitated by an epidemic resulting from the lack of a public sewage system could hardly be considered free for self development.

Green came to see that liberty must not be merely negative (freedom *from* governmental interference). It must be positive as well—freedom *for* development. Naturally, moral or intellectual development cannot be legislated because it is the act or character of a free agent, but it is possible to create conditions under which it can occur. Not the least important is freedom from compulsion by others. Therefore, Green held that while government cannot make people moral by law, their moral development can be achieved by removing hindrances. Politics then was essentially an agency for creating social conditions which made moral development possible.

Thus, organic liberalism maintained its adherence to individual freedom and equality but differed from earlier liberal thought on the proper function of government. Organic liberalism allowed a positive, active function in opposition to the earlier liberal emphasis on *laissez faire*. This was a breakthrough in liberal thought in relation to poverty, which, finally, was a legitimate public policy subject—as long as it allowed individuals to develop without interfering with their rights to seek private ends. Liberals who recognized the problems of poor people need not scrap capitalism, just soften its harsh edges.

COMPARISONS AND CONTRASTS

While organic liberalism shared an organic view of society, with conservatism and socialism, it differed on key issues. Marxian socialism attributed social life and development entirely to economic factors, assuming class war. In contrast, organic liberalism shared with conservatism a conception of society as a whole in which all parts interacted and in which economic factors were only part of the explanation of social life and development. Whereas conservatism stressed hierarchy and inequality, organic liberalism was founded on free individuals, capable of growth. Unlike conservatism or socialism, organic liberalism maintained that individuals should be free to seek private ends, and assumed that men were both capable of rational choice and shared similar needs and goals that could be the basis of public policy. With regard to poverty policy, socialism and liberalism differed: socialists defined poverty in relative terms, requiring massive redistribution of wealth and state ownership of the means of production; organic liberalism defined poverty as a question of subsistence. To be free for moral development men needed not only subsistence but also protection, such as factory safety laws, wage and hour laws, pure food and drug laws, public health and sanitation laws, and education. Consequently, these and similar needs were appropriate subjects for public policy. However, the state could not regulate individuals beyond the necessities for individual growth and development. Thus, private enterprise was acceptable to organic liberals, as were large differences in the distribution of individual wealth.

AMERICAN MATERIALISTIC INDIVIDUALISM

American political thought has been dominated by the liberal tradition.[12] Its implications for the poor may be seen in the easy equation that John Locke was able to make between moral worth and material riches. His theory of property provided a "positive moral basis for capitalist society," by asserting that an individual's property was his own and (unlike his right to life or liberty) might be alienated through a wage contract.[13] Also, Locke considered class differential in rights and rationality to be natural.[14] Since he viewed unemployment as the result of moral depravity, he advocated such measures as using workhouses for forced-labor manufacturing, and putting all children of the unemployed above the age of three to work, to earn more than their keep.[15]

Frontier conditions of a new country consistently reinforced settlers' materialistic individualism. Rugged entrepreneurial activity and exploitation of natural and human resources were the rule. Of necessity, frontier life placed a premium on indivdual action and self-reliance. At the core of this individualism lay: "a materialistic philosophy. which enshrined property rights and held them to be largely immune from governmental or public control."[16] Under harsh frontier conditions, where even the basic amenities of civilized life were not readily available, public concern for the unemployed and poor were minimal. Poverty was equated with personal failure.

The equation of moral worth with material possessions found in liberalism and reinforced by frontier conditions was also part of the major religious tradition during the nation's formative period. Calvinist thought shaped the values of most of the early settlers of America, including English Pilgrims and Puritans, French Huguenots, Scots, and the Dutch. Although the tradition of Christian thought had included concepts of love for one's neighbor, sharing one's goods with the less fortunate, the brotherhood of all men, and the community of all believers, Christianity's primary emphasis had been placed on the individual. The soul's salvation has been its paramount concern, yet salvation could only be accomplished individually through a person's faith and/or good works. Thus, while important, charity and community have tended to be secondary factors in Christian thought, functioning as signs of the individual believer's inner grace and/or a means to his salvation.

Calvinism relegated them to an even lower level of significance, thereby indirectly enhancing the individualistic aspects of Christian thought. Calvin had maintained that salvation depended on the inscrutable will of God that had foreordained salvation for some and damnation for others. In *practice*, his followers generally assumed that earthly prosperity indicated God's favor and was therefore a sign of future grace. Thus, the majority of early colonists brought to America an individualism which directly correlated moral worth with material prosperity. As Max Weber indicated, Protestantism (particularly the Calvinist persuasion) was closely allied to capitalism and provided a rationale and defense for the system.[17] So poverty was viewed as a sign of individual moral weakness. Measures to deal with the poor were harsh and condemnatory: public work house, debtor's prison, or loss of a hand for theft of bread. Only the most limited measures were taken to assist destitute widows, orphans, or the mentally or physically handicapped.

The era following the Civil War was characterized by America's industrial revolution. Americans experienced the extraordinary economic benefits and social costs of rapid industrialization, urbanization, exploitation of the nation's natural resources on an unforseen scale, the close of the frontier, and imperialistic adventures in the Caribbean and Philippines. These developments seemed to necessitate, and were supported by, a philosophical apotheosis of materialistic individualism that combined *laissez faire* capitalist theories with social analogies and produced Social Darwinism—Darwin's evolutionary theory of survival of the fittest applied to human society.

Darwin's theory had been morally neutral: the fact that long-necked giraffes survived while those with short-necks perished simply indicated the survival of the fittest in terms of environmental adaptation. Ethics or esthetics had no bearing on the fact. However, when applied to society, Darwinian concepts generally bore moral connotations as well. Since most American Protestant and constitutional thought had traditionally been skeptical of the moral worth of the poor, it found little difficulty in assimilating these concepts. The reason for the widespread popularity from 1865 to 1890 of Herbert Spencer's justification of individualism and hostility to government regulation might be found in the fact that it "powerfully reinforced ideas that were already fairly strong and put them on a seemingly scientific basis."[18]

In America these ideas were pushed to their logical extreme by William Graham Sumner, who maintained that there could be no possibility of social reform as human intelligence was inadequate to deal with such problems. Therefore, man should allow free play to the forces of nature. Sumner's links to earlier American thought were indicated by one analyst in the following terms: "Like some latter-day Calvin, he came to preach the predestination of the social order and the salvation of the economically elect through the survival of the fittest."[19]

The harsh implications of Sumner's theory for the poor are obvious. And most Protestant churches did not soften them by a counter emphasis on charity. Social Darwinism was the justification for the business community's actions which business accepted; and the Protestant Churches supported business, providing "religious sanction for the businessman's views with respect to property, inequality, stewardship, state aid and labor."[20] Taking a negative view of social reform and state action, they stressed individual regeneration. While the popular Baptist minister, Russell H. Conwell, may have been unusual for the frequency of his speeches (the same speech 6,000 times) his sentiments were widely held and propounded from other pulpits. Proclaiming the intriguing theory that it was a Christian's duty to get rich because more could be done with money than without, he held that the poor were the victims of their own shortcomings: "It is all wrong to be poor."[21]

Ironically, many American businessmen seemed more inclined to soften the harsh edge of Sumner's theory toward the poor than did these clergymen. In *The Gospel of Wealth* the major industrialist of his day, Andrew Carnegie, advocated using wealth consciously for the general welfare but this would be done on the basis of a "trustee-ship" held by the wealthy and used at their discretion, such as Carnegie lending libraries. The implications of such "softening" doctrines were demonstrated by a journalist who cloaked the barbs of his social criticism behind the humorous creation of conversations with a sage Irish barkeep, Mr. Dooley:

"Has Andhrew Carnaygie given ye a libry yet?" asked Mr. Dooley.
"Not that I know iv," said Mr. Hennessy.
"He will," said Mr. Dooley. "Ye'll not escape him. Befure he dies he hopes to crowd a libry on ivry man, woman, an' child in th' coonthry. . . . No beggar is iver turned impty-handed fr'm th' dure. Th' pan-handler knocks an' asts f'r a glass iv milk an' a roll. 'No, sir,' says Andhrew Carnaygie. 'I will not pauperize this unworthy man. Nawthin' is worse f'r a beggar-man thin to make a pauper iv him. Yet it shall not be said iv me that I give nawthin' to th' poor. Saunders, give him a libry, . . .'"
"Does he give th' books that go with it?" asked Mr. Hennessy.
"Books?" said Mr. Dooley. "What ar-re ye talkin' about? D'ye know what a libry is? . . . A Carnaygie libry is a large, brown-stone, impenethrible buildin' with th' name iv th' maker blown on th' dure. . . . A Carnaygie libry is archytechooor, not lithrachoor. . . . Carnegie says that "Th' worst thing we can do f'r anny man is to do him good. . . .'"

". . . Him that giveth to th' poor, they say, lindeth to th' Lord; but in these days we look f'r quick returns on our invistments. . . ."[22]

The exploitative and harsh aspects of Social Darwinism became increasingly apparent as the century progressed, resulting in a growing awareness that there was a contradiction between the materialistic premises and individual freedom. American critics of Social Darwinism responded in two ways—socialism or progressivism. Spokesmen for a form of socialism stimulated popular debate and fear, but made little headway against dominant values. Far more successful attacks on Social Darwinism were waged by Populists led by William Jennings Bryan, and by Progressives. These included Herbert Croly, Theodore Roosevelt, Louis Brandeis, Woodrow Wilson, and Robert LaFollette (both senior and junior) whose values corresponded with the dominant American preference for materialistic individualism. They were essentially ambivalent, combining a *laissez-faire* attack on trusts, monopolies, and party bosses with some organic liberal reforms to ease urban blight and poverty. The struggle to combine the two philosophies lasted for several decades, during which *laissez-faire* was emphasized. The New Deal era marked the successful emergence of organic liberalism as a major American ideology. Nevertheless, the struggle to combine *laissez-faire* and organic liberalism persisted well into F.D.R.'s second term, and his actions were more a matter of expedient response to crisis than the reflection of an organic liberal ideology.

Thus, the New Deal philosophy departed very little from materialistic individualism; nor have government programs to date significantly altered the situation, contrary to widespread public rhetoric that America has entered an era of "creeping socialism." Organic liberalism is not socialism. In the American context most "conservatives" are actually liberals who retain allegiance to the *laissez-faire* liberalism of Adam Smith, whereas "liberals" stress positive as well as negative freedom. Both American "conservatives" and "liberals" agree on the value of human freedom to pursue private ends, but disagree on the function that government should play in the process. While some Burkean conservatives and some Marxian socialists coexist, both groups have been too small to have had much influence on American public policy.

Throughout its history the value of materialistic individualism has held a dominant position in American political thought, shaping the concept within which public policy toward the poor has been formulated.

Ethnocentrism, another pervasive American value, has also affected public policy decisions. As a result, persons who have not been Protestants of northwestern European origins, particularly not Caucasian, disproportionately compose the poor in America. As has been stated, over a third of the nation's poor are nonwhite, although other races constitute only a sixth of the entire population. Thus, racism is of particular significance for poverty policy. Ethnocentrism, whose cutting edge for the poor is racism, is partially defined:

eth-no-cen-trism 1) a habitual disposition to judge foreign peoples or groups by the standards and practices of one's own culture or ethnic groups. . . . 2) a tendency toward viewing alien cultures with disfavor and a resulting sense of inherent superiority.[23]

All nations have been, more or less, ethnocentric, especially America. From its inception until the nineteenth century the "promised land," the "new" world, the "New Jerusalem," was populated primarily by white Protestants of northwestern European origins. Their middle class and wealthy members framed and controlled the governmental, social, and economic institutions. Black men were merely considered property in a large part of the country until the Civil War, and hardly perceived as equals thereafter.

Catholic refugees from Ireland and southern Germany experienced violent prejudice and repression, as did East European Jews. Some of the major organizations whose aim was repressing Catholics and Jews include the national Know-Nothing Party of the 1840s and 1850s (which "enlivened" the public scene by such acts as burning convents), the anti-Semitism and anti-Catholicism of the Ku Klux Klan which organized after the Civil War and the Populist movement of the 1890s. When the Irish finally gained political power in Eastern urban centers by capturing the "machine" in the late nineteenth and early twentieth centuries, their opponents, the Progressives, were greatly strengthened by the anti-Catholic sentiments of Progressive supporters who were primarily middle class white Protestants of northwestern European stock.[24] All succeeding immigrant groups that were not white, and of northern European stock have experienced persistent discrimination and often persecution for their religious, cultural, and racial differences from the dominant group, which has maintained control of the government, business, and industry.

JUSTIFICATION OF CONCEPTS

During the nineteenth century, as other ethnics migrated to America, the basic prejudices of its ruling class were strengthened and "justified" by several developments in scientific and social thought. Concepts of "survival of the fittest" race, and fear of race "mongrelization" were increasingly voiced in private, public, and governmental circles. These beliefs were strongly buttressed by widespread acceptance of "scientific proof" based on the work of the French naturalist, Jean Baptiste Lamarck, who introduced a theory of evolution that appeared to add the stamp of "scientific objectivity" to ethnocentrism and imperialistic expansion. The theory, which was influential during the last quarter of the eighteenth century and first quarter of the nineteenth, consisted of the idea (totally discredited by further research) that an organism "passes to offspring the characteristics developed because of a need created by its environment."[25] This theory of genetic transmission of acquired characteristics influenced the father of Social Darwinism, Herbert Spencer and confirmed his evolutionary optimism: "For if mental as well as physical characteristics could be inherited, the intellectual powers of the race would become cumulatively greater, and over several generations the ideal man would finally be developed."[26]

This mutually reinforcing relationship between Social Darwinism and concepts of acquired characteristics through inheritance provided the theoretical justification for the raw imperialism entailed in the idea of "Manifest Destiny." That doctrine skillfully blended the primary American values of materialistic individualism and ethnocentrism into a justification for world domination on the ground that Americans were "in charge of the final theatre and the final problems of history."[27] The *New York Daily News* editorial from which that quotation of the 1850s was taken represented editorial and public sentiments widely expressed throughout the land:

Our hearts beat for an oppressed world. Our object is the greatest good of all men. We believe that our Government is best calculated to make men happy, and that it can be extended over a continent or a world. . . . What hinders, we ask, a Government like this from extending over the world and making it politically happy?[28]

Such a conclusion synthesized the arrogant optimism that had dominated American thought for generations until the aftermath of World War I, which did *not* make the world "safe for democary." The Great Depression began on a wide scale to undermine such simple faith. "Manifest Destiny" thus became America's justification for Indian genocide as the side effect of conquering the continent. It justified America's relations with Mexico, Central America, the Caribbean Islands, and the Pacific Islands, such as the Samoan Islands, the Hawaiian Islands, the Philippines and Guam.[29] Ethnocentrism was also the basis for the restrictive immigration policy that developed from the 1880s until 1965. Complete exclusion of orientals was accomplished prior to World War I, and by 1924 immigration quotas were imposed *explicitly* to curtail immigration from southern and southeastern Europe.[30] These ethnic quotas did not end until 1965.

While "Manifest Destiny" has dropped from public favor, ethnocentrism has continued to dominate American thought and action, and has left all nonwhite groups in a disadvantaged position. Even the Irish, who have been here longer than any other group but the dominant one, have not benefited proportionally, despite occasional conspicuous exceptions, such as the Kennedys and the Buckleys. Many Americans have felt and still feel that this ethnocentrism has limited their opportunities. At the end of the 1960s nation-wide Gallup polls indicated rising discontent and organization among disadvantaged ethnic groups.[31] For example, the 1970 picketing of F.B.I. headquarters by sponsors of Italian Unity Day was an expression of antagonism to government policy.

Use of racist fears has been one means through which the dominant group has maintained power. Particularly in the South, the use of racist fears has been a traditional and highly effective way to pit low status people against each other, thereby diffusing their potential for attacking those in control. Thus, for example, in his landmark study of Southern state politics, V.O. Key found that the question was not so much one of white control, but the control of upper class whites. They used racism to keep poor whites from combining with poor blacks to gain improved state services, thereby maintaining a low wage, low tax, nonunion economy from which the formulators of that public policy benefited.[32]

Recent research indicates that working class Caucasians who are not of Protestant or northwestern European origin, need to find a lower status group (the poor or nonwhites) to provide them with a sense of status in a society dominated by what are popularly called WASPS (white, Anglo-Saxon Protestants—the term is used loosely to apply to all white Protestants of northwestern European stock, not just the Anglo-Saxons). Despite rhetoric concerning human equality, Robert Lane's study of white (but primarily non-WASP) American working men found that:

. . . these men, by and large, prefer an inequalitarian society, and even prefer a society graced by some men of great wealth. . . . their life goals are structured around achievement and success in monetary terms.[33]

His study found that greater equality of opportunity and income were actually psychologically threatening, as it would result in problems of social adjustment and the loss of life goals for men whose society emphasized consumption. The rise of ethnic group organization and militance at the end of the 1960s and beginning of the 1970s was indicative of the status disorientation produced by gains in black status, which had resulted from a decade of civil rights agitation.

Consequently, while ethnocentrism explains the disadvantaged position of all non-WASP groups in America, its expression in racism has been its cutting edge for the poor. All Caucasian groups have combined in antagonism to other races, with the result that the poor in America have been disproportionately nonwhite. Studies show that it is primarily racism that explains (and has been used to justify) the conditions of blacks, Indians, Mexicans, Puerto Ricans and Orientals in America.[34]

RACISM TOWARD BLACKS

Although a few individuals at the nation's inception took egalitarianism under natural law seriously, majority opinion was profoundly racist. Therefore, Congress expeditiously dropped the passage from Jefferson's original draft of the Declaration of Independence that explicitly condemned black slavery.[35] It was published with no reference to abolition. Nor did the Constitution remain silent on this question. It recognized, accepted, and indirectly legitimized black slavery by counting slaves as three-fifths of a free man for purposes of apportioning representation,[36] and by denying states the right to prohibit migration and importation of slaves for twenty years.[37] Enslavement of blacks remained the pattern for a sizable part of the nation until the Civil War, but even the citizens of free states who advocated abolition were racist in their underlying assumptions. For example, in a speech advocating abolition Abraham Lincoln said:

There is a natural disgust in the minds of nearly all white people at the idea of indiscriminate amalgamation of the white and black races; . . . I protest against the counterfeit logic which concludes that, because I do not want a black woman for a slave I must necessarily want her for a wife. I need not have her for either. I can just leave her alone. In some respects she certainly is not my equal; but in her natural right to eat bread she earns with her own hands without asking leave of anyone else, she is my equal, and the equal of all others.[38]

Following the Civil War a system of Jim Crow laws totally segregating the races developed in the South and was given Constitutional respectability by the United States Supreme Court in the case of *Plessy v. Ferguson.* They were justified or "explained" on myriad grounds ranging from Biblical interpretation to pseudo-scientific theories of inherent genetic incapacity.[39] Not until the Plessy doctrine was reversed by the 1954 Supreme Court holding in the case of *Brown v. the Board of Education of Topeka* was Constitutional legitimacy removed from racial discrimination. However, attitudes and opinions widely voiced to the present day are similar to those voiced a century earlier.[40] Thus, stereotypes structure American thought.

Although most Americans are partially aware of the nation's heritage of racism with respect to blacks, they tend conveniently to view it more as an isolated and unusual historical accident rather than as a single demonstration of a fundamental value pervasive throughout American society. Such selective perception is necessary in order to preserve the comforting self-image inculcated through daily compulsory repetition in the nation's schools of the Pledge of Allegiance which alleges that the United States is ". . . one nation . . . with liberty and justice for all."

Vicious as has been the impact of racism on the black man, it has had even more devastating impact on the Indian. It also structures the life patterns of Mexican-Americans, Puerto Ricans on the mainland, and Orientals. A brief consideration of the manner in which these less known groups are affected must dispel any comforting illusions that the condition of blacks does not reflect the values of the dominant culture but is an historical aberration.

RACISM TOWARD INDIANS

The American Indian has been the object of the nation's most virulent racist policy, as a few examples indicate. Antagonism toward Indians was as effective a means to a political career in the nineteenth century as was a segregationist platform in most parts of the South until quite recently. For example, Andrew Jackson's presidential aspirations had been enhanced by slaughter of Creeks and Seminoles; Benjamin Harrison was remembered primarily for an attack on an Indian village at Tippecanoe. Using the slogan of his victory, rather than his name, which was hardly a household word, Harrison sought and won the Presidency in 1840 with his running mate John Tyler: "Tippecanoe and Tyler Too!" And Abraham Lincoln's primary military experience was as an Indian fighter in the Black Hawk War of 1832.

Americans frequently abrogated or failed to honor treaties with Indian tribes and rarely supported them in courts of law. In fact, it was in the context of a rare decision by the Supreme Court in *favor* of Indian rights that President Andrew Jackson was alleged to have made his famous statement about the Chief Justice: "John Marshall has made his decision, now let him enforce it."

Indians were repeatedly killed under a flag of truce. Repeatedly "good" citizens got "likkered up" and went out to slaughter a nearby encampment of women and children while braves were hunting. Tippecanoe, for example, was an attack by Harrison, in violation of orders, on a village populated by old men and women. Custer's last stand was made in a battle brought about by such a slaughter. All of these actions were legitimized on the ground that promises to inferiors did not matter, and that the only good Indian was a dead Indian. Therefore, the notorious, widespread graft in the federal agencies regulating Indian affairs, prevalent particularly after the Civil War, attracted little public censure. Indicative of the widespread attitude that Indians were subhuman animals was the invasion after 1871 of their burial grounds for bones for button manufacturers.[41]

It is a plain fact of American history, unselfconsciously *celebrated* by almost every school textbook and a large body of American literature, films, and programs for the mass media, that Caucasian Americans engaged in acts of genocide with regard to the indigenous Indian population. By 1900 they had reduced the Indian population of aboriginal times to *one-sixteenth* through warfare, the various treks of tribes resulting from several "Indian removal" laws, malnutrition and disease on those treks and on the reservations to which Indians were sent. For example, only about one-half of the Creek people survived its removal to the Indian Territory in 1836, 4,000 Cherokees died in their 1838 removal ("Trail of Tears"). Similarly, one-half of the Winnebago tribe was destroyed in 1840; only one-tenth of California's Mission Indians survived. Not to be forgotten was the high death toll from "The Long Walk" taken by Navahoes and Apaches in 1864, and from the Nez Percé removal in 1877.

Bill Cody's nickname, Buffalo Bill, came from his single-handed slaughter of over 4,000 buffalo, a major source of food and leather (for clothing and shelter) for the plains Indians. (Since buffalo propagate very slowly, such slaughter contributed to the near extinction of the species.) Reservation life further destroyed the people and culture.[42]

To the present day racist attitudes toward American Indians pervade American culture and are unselfconsciously promoted as "history" and "entertainment." For example, an extraordinary level of bloodshed and violence against Indians has been condoned in television and films, as part of the American frontier mythology. This popular culture has thus socialized urban American youth in the last half of the twentieth century with the same racial stereotype toward Indians that was prevalent a century or two earlier. Such attitudes have affected public policy toward Indians in many ways which have maintained and perpetuated their poverty.

RACISM TOWARD HISPANO-AMERICANS

Another major group experiencing America's racial prejudice are the Hispano-Americans comprising approximately four million Mexican-Americans and about one million Puerto Ricans living on the mainland.[43] In addition to racial discrimination, they must cope with prejudice stemming from their religious and cultural traditions. Predominantly Roman Catholic, they experience the anti-Catholicism that has been prevalent throughout America's history. Because they speak a language other than English, they are handicapped in the only industrial nation in the world in which a person who just speaks one language is considered educated. They have also been discriminated against because of their cultural traditions which are not northwest European. Mexican-

Americans found that early land grants were not protected in the courts, and that much of their land was taken illegally. United States government policy further limited their grazing land by turning vast tracts of New Mexico into Forest Reserve land and recreation centers for visitors. Consequently, residents must not only pay for permits to keep livestock but they are closely regulated as to the number and type of animals they can keep. These restrictions deepen their state of poverty.

RACISM TOWARD ORIENTALS

Discrimination against Orientals has been an aspect of American public policy on national, state, and local levels since substantial immigration began in the nineteenth century. Orientals were the first targets of the nation's early immigration restrictions: Chinese excluded in 1882, Japanese in 1907. Americans assumed as a matter of course that Orientals were inferiors, who, "lacking Christianity, democracy, and the steam engine, had to be taught proper western ways of doing things."[44] For example, the diary of Townsend Harris, first American Consul General to Japan, unselfconsciously proclaimed a virulent sense of racism toward the Japanese and an unyielding belief in his country's "Manifest Destiny" to impose its will upon them. These attitudes were continually reflected in his actions.[45]

As thousands of Chinese were imported for cheap labor to build the vast railroad network which made possible settlement and exploitation of the continent, public hysteria also mounted toward this "yellow peril." By 1890, despite exclusion laws and feelings of "sinophobia," there were an estimated 102,620 Chinese residents in America, concentrated on the West Coast, especially in California.[46] The extraordinarily high ratio of men to women, 27 men to one woman, in the context of a racist nation that ghettoized non-Caucasians and applied legal, economic, and social sanctions to prevent their having sexual relations with Caucasian females, led to behavior patterns that reinforced the hostile stereotypes of their neighbors. Chinese men responded to their imposed isolation by forming clans and secret societies for identity, and by escaping through prostitutes, opium, and gambling.[47] Their enclaves then came to fill the role for white society that black ghettoes have traditionally filled: supplier of illicit pleasures that served the dual function of satisfying white desire while gratifying white perceptions that the suppliers were a morally inferior race.

The Chinese who tried to avoid that situation were faced with almost insuperable legal barriers and administrative harassment, such as the California land laws that prohibited orientals from purchasing or owning land in the state. These laws even extended to prohibiting such possession by the children of American-born Orientals who were subject to its laws. This was based on the racist presumption that they could not be considered American citizens. In 1898 a Supreme Court decision declared it unconstitutional, upholding the principle that birth in the United States conferred citizenship on the children of alien parents, even if the parents themselves were ineligible for citizenship.[48]

A major expression of blatant racism toward Orientals in America was the Japanese Relocation Program during World War II.[49] Prior to the war, the Justice Department had investigated all enemy aliens and citizens (German, Italian, and Japanese) on an individual basis and classified them for security purposes. Those considered "dangerous" were arrested on an individual basis at the outbreak of hostilities. The F.B.I. and Justice Department firmly maintained that it was not necessary for national security to treat Japanese and Japanese-Americans any differently than German or Italian aliens or citizens.

Mounting hysteria on the West Coast found an influential spokesman in General John L. DeWitt, Commanding Officer of the Fourth Army and Western Defense Command. Through the War Department, he and sympathizers battled the Justice Department for responsibility in the area. Eventually, President Roosevelt capitulated, and Executive Order 9066, issued in February 1942, transferred control over these matters to the War Department. General DeWitt then shipped Japanese and American citizens of Japanese descent to concentration camps in the desert and, euphemistically, labeled them "Relocation Centers." (Caucasian aliens, Germans, and Italians, nor their American-born offspring, were never treated in such a manner.) As a result Japanese stores were looted, property was sold cheaply in public auction because its owners had failed to pay taxes during their internment, and land was appropriated, particularly in California. Ironically, any of these assumedly "subversive" citizens who wished to die for their country could serve in segregated units in the Armed Forces. Many earned great distinction for combat bravery while their families were interned. Further irony was witnessed in Hawaii. Much closer to Japan, recipient of an actual air attack, and with a far larger Japanese population than the West Coast, Hawaii never treated Asians in this way nor underwent this hysteria. The primary difference between Hawaii and the mainland was the fact that only ten percent of Hawaii's population was Caucasian, which limited their capacity to inflict their values on other races.

The fear of a "yellow peril" was resurrected after the war in a new guise. For example, a recent speech by F.B.I. Director J. Edgar Hoover suggested a categorical approach to the Chinese that was never applied to Caucasian aliens or their descendants from communist states, although these Caucasians have been far more numerous than the Chinese. In the fall of 1969, Chinese-Americans picketed F.B.I. Headquarters in New York to protest Hoover's statement to a U.S. House of Representatives subcommittee that the F.B.I. had a growing amount of work being alert to Chinese Americans, on the assumption that the Chinese would most likely help the Communist cause because of their origin.[50]

CONCLUSION TO DATE

Thus, ethnocentrism (particularly racism) has been a pervasive American value. In conjunction with the value of materialistic individualism, it has caused members of the minority groups just discussed to face *double* jeopardy. American racism has led to discriminatory practices which have *caused* them to be disproportionately represented among the poor.[51] Then, as a consequence of American devotion to materialistic individualism, these people have been further discriminated against *because* they were poor.

The values of materialistic individualism and ethnocentrism have severely limited the degree to which Americans have been willing to consider poverty as a legitimate subject for public policy, and narrowly restricted the alternative policies which have been acceptable to the American electorate. They also have had an impact on the self-image of the poor themselves, inhibiting their development of alternatives apart from those provided by the mainstream.

RESULTING PUBLIC ATTITUDES TOWARD THE POOR

The dominant values of materialistic individualism and ethnocentrism (particularly racism) have led to stereotyped public attitudes toward the poor, especially the nonwhite poor, which have been highly resistant to change.

PUBLIC ATTITUDES TOWARD POOR PEOPLE

These stereotypes have grown from and reinforced materialistic individualism as was shown in Robert Lane's in-depth study of the belief structure of the "comman man":

If one accepts the view that this is a land of opportunity in which merit will find a way, one is encouraged to accept the status differences of society. . . . There are satisfactions of identification with the going social order; it is easier to accept differences one calls "just" than those that appear "unjust"; there are the very substantial self-congratulatory satisfactions of comparison with those lower on the scale. Thus this theme of "just deserts" applies to one's own group, those higher and those lower.[52]

The characteristics of the attitudes of working men toward the poor was similar to that found by Adam Walinsky's analysis of the status-anxiety of middle-class Americans in general. In discussing the myths held by middle-class Americans particularly about the poor he wrote:

In present-day America, the middle class is defined largely by the fact that the poor exist. Doctors are middle class, but so are bookkeepers; factory workers vacation with lawyers, drive bigger cars than teachers, live next door to store-owners, and send their children to school with the children of bank tellers. In a middle class so diffuse, with almost no characteristic common to all, middle-class income, education and housing are what the poor do not have. If the present poor should become middle class, no meaning would remain to the phrase; . . . The middle class knows that the economists are right when they say that poverty can be eliminated if we only will it; they simply do not will it. . . .

I suspect that the tension between adherence to democratic ideals and a natural desire to preserve one's relative gains by denying them to others has been heightened by a general loss of middle-class security [due to] enlargement in the size of the middle class itself: by the social and economic elevation of production and service workers; by the slackening of immigration, which has produced an America 95 per cent native-born and thus eliminated much "native" prestige; by the spread of education, high school and now college; by the general availability of inexpensive goods (especially clothing) virtually identical to those used by the well-to-do. For the old middle class, this has meant a dilution of status, which they have attempted to recapture by shifting the criteria of middle-class membership from income ("mere money") to sophistication of various sorts—education, community service, culture. For the new middle class, the gain in status is precarious; they attempt to reinforce it by appropriating the symbols of the old middle class, especially suburban housing and education for the children. For both old and new middle classes, the problem of preserving status becomes more acute in direct proportion to the technical ease with which poverty can be eliminated from the country. . . .[53]

Such attitudes have led to the pervasive acceptance of poverty apparent in polls conducted about 30 years apart by the American Institute of Public Opinion. In response to the question, "Do you think that poverty will ever be done away with in this country?" it found:[54]

Table 2.1

		Yes	No	No Opinion
1937	(August 16)	13%	83%	4%
1964	(March 22)	9%	83%	8%

The same attitudes are also linked to the pervading cynicism about both those on relief, and the poor in general. They have created a self-serving mythology concerning the poor and welfare, based on belief in the moral unworthiness of these people. And they have reinforced that belief. The basic myths are: the poor have children in order to get welfare; there are large numbers of able-bodied men who loaf while on welfare; they buy the luxuries for which the middle class must work.

None of these myths is sustained by fact. For example, social science research conducted during the past five years shows that having children for welfare eligibility is a figment of middle-class imagination. Since welfare payments start at an inadequate subsistence level and diminish with each additional child, they have been hardly a motherhood incentive. In fact, welfare mother's polls indicate that the poor, especially blacks and Puerto Ricans, *want* less children than higher status Caucasians. Between 70 and 90 percent of recipients interviewed in various studies said they not only wished to obtain contraceptive information and devices but also wished to terminate their pregnancies and wanted no more children. Ironically, "the ladies with really ambitious fertility attitudes these days are the suburban ladies, not the ones of the city slums."[55]

Similarly, the stated myth that large numbers of able-bodied men loaf while on the welfare rolls is selective perception by the general public. For example, in 1967, of the 7.3 million U.S. welfare recipients, 2.1 million were 65 years or older (mostly women), 3.5 million were children under 18 years, 900,000 were mothers of these children and 150,000 were men between 18 and 65, two-thirds of whom were incapacitated. Thus, only 50,000, or *less than one percent* of America's welfare recipients, were even potentially employable males, and the vast majority lacked available jobs, training, skills and/or education necessary to obtain employment.[56]

Only about one *half* of those presently *eligible* actually receive welfare payments. On the assumption that there is widespread cheating, a high percentage of welfare costs are used to finance investigations. More dollars are spent per year for investigations in this area than for programs such as Project Headstart. Results have hardly justified their expense, but they continue because Americans believe that the poor are morally unworthy and consequently *must* be cheating. Two recently well publicized investigations in New York State indicate this discrepancy. After an intensive (and expensive) investigation, the city of Newburgh found two employable males on relief; Auburn found one, who died of a heart attack, on his first day of work, shoveling snow for the city.

One of the other myths, that welfare recipients own luxuries for which the middle class must work, is obviously absurd, though psychologically gratifying. Actually, the poor *own* almost nothing. Their "possessions" are obtained on credit at exorbitant interest rates. Ghetto inhabitants also do not have access to local stores with competitive prices or good merchandise, so they receive inferior quality at inflated prices. The extraordinary level of financial victimization of the poor has been well documented by private and public investigations.[57] Although none of these myths is sustained by fact, their influence is powerful because they are rooted in and support basic American values of materialistic individualism. The myths have increased racial hostility because "they" tend to be perceived as primarily nonwhite.

The inadequacy of welfare payments also is a reflection of the wide-spread American equation of material possession with moral worth: If the poor are unworthy, then it is not obligatory to care for them. Any giving in itself is commendable, thus the fact that one gives to the poor is proof of his moral superiority. The adequacy of support is an irrelevant question. In many states, welfare payments have been hopelessly inadequate for minimum standards of health and decency.[58] For example, to a mother with three dependent children in 1969 the State of Mississippi paid a monthly check averaging $38.05—or under $10 per month for each family member. The average *national* welfare payment to a mother with three dependent children was $171 per month or under $43 per month for each family member. This equaled $513 per person per year—tantamount to slow starvation in America. Even the most generous state, New York, provided the same family with approximately $249.75 per month, or $60 per person per month—a sum barely adequate for survival in New York City. Furthermore, frequently eligibility requirements have been so arranged that the destitute cannot get aid at all, or not in time.

SELECTIVE PERCEPTION ON RACE

Selective perception of white, middle-class Americans has been particularly evident in considering members of other races. Whites have not perceived the realities of life that other races have experienced and, therefore, generally, have ignored their problems. Since blacks have been the largest racial minority in America, and have received the greatest attention in opinion studies, they are used as an example of the plight of non-Caucasians. Because, as previously indicated, America's poor have been disproportionately nonwhite, the discrepancies between their experience and the view of life by the middle-class white majority have particular importance.

A broad Gallup survey of white attitudes in 1969 revealed that whites felt that blacks were receiving too much, too quickly. In response to the question, "Do Negroes today have a better chance or worse chance than people like yourself?", the following responses reflected white perceptions:[59]

Table 2.2

	Better	Worse	Same
To get well paying jobs?	44%	21%	31%
To get a good education for their children?	41	16	41
To get good housing at a reasonable cost?	35	30	27
To get financial help from the government when they're out of work?	65	4	22

While these were the responses of whites as a whole, blue collar whites were particularly concerned about blacks. Nearly half, 49 percent, believed that blacks had a better chance to get a good job than they did; one-third said that black demands were unjustified.[60] Blacks had a different viewpoint. In contrasting earlier polls of blacks with one taken in 1967 Gallup found that blacks had a *growing* perception that they were being discriminated against in America: ". . . . that he pays higher prices and more rent than whites, that he is paid lower wages for equal work, that he has less chance at college and the really good jobs. . . ."[61] It found that bitterness, alienation, and despair among blacks had increased, while 59 percent found the pace of change too slow.

Such discrepancies between black and white perceptions of reality are not new. Research data over the past decade have indicated similar differences,[62] as have studies of local areas.[63]

In the context of objective evidence collected by the U.S. Bureau of the Census, it is clear that black perception is far more realistic than that of whites. While the 1970 census showed some increase in both income and opportunity for blacks, their income, education, housing, and health were still disproportionate among the poor. Among other studies, the 1968 Koerner Commission report on civil disorders documented the degree to which racial discrimination has continued to block equal job, housing, or educational opportunities. It concluded: "Our nation is moving toward two societies—one black, one white; separate and unequal."[64] This particular report was upheld by a private study of American cities entitled "One Year Later." It found that: "We are one year closer to two societies—black and white, increasingly separate and scarcely less equal."[65]

The most extreme examples of selective perception and stereotyped thinking regarding racial questions have occurred in the South. A recent major study found that the South was divided into two hostile groups on the pivotal question of segregation and that neither group correctly estimated the views of the other. Moreover, the situation was deteriorating because of mutual underestimation of the seriousness of the conflict.[66]

In summary, the attitudes of the majority of Americans have demonstrated pervasive stereotyped thinking and selective perception toward all the poor, particularly toward racial minorities. This has been reflected throughout the nation's history in its public policy toward the poor, and in the practices and procedures of the professions upon which the poor depend, as will be further considered in Chapters Three and Four.

Notes

1. For a concise analysis of the development of the liberal tradition see L. T. HOB-HOUSE, *Liberalism* (Oxford: Oxford University Press, 1964).

2. JOHN LOCKE, *The Social Contract* (1690).

3. DAVID HUME, *Treatise on Human Nature* (1737).

4. ADAM SMITH, *The Wealth of Nations* (1776).

5. EDMUND BURKE, *Reflections on the Revolution in France* (1790).

6. JOSEPH DE MAISTRE, *Considerations on France* (1796).

7. LOUIS DE BONALD, *On Primitive Legislation* (1802).

8. JOHANN FICHTE, *Address to the German Nation* (1808).

9. Three principal groups developed this theory: in France, Henry de Rouvroy, Comte de Saint-Simon (1760–1820) with the Saint Simonians, and Charles Fourier (1772–1827) with the Fourierists; in England, Robert Owen (1771–1859) and the Owenites. For a concise analysis of the utopian socialists see G.D.H. COLE, *A History of Socialist Thought* (New York: Macmillan, 1959), vol. I.

10. KARL MARX and FRIEDRICH ENGELS, *The German Ideology* (1846), and *Communist Manifesto* (1848), KARL MARX, *Das Kapital* (1867) and *The Civil War in France* (1871).

11. T. H. GREEN, *Principles of Political Organization* (1882).

12. For opposite poles agreeing on this point see LOUIS HARTZ, *The Liberal Tradition in America* (New York: Harcourt, Brace and World, 1955), and CLINTON ROSSITER, *Conservation in America* (New York: Vintage, 1962).

13. C. B. MACPHERSON, *The Political Theory of Possessive Individualism* (London: Oxford University Press, 1962), p. 221.

14. These views appear in several works. See particularly JOHN LOCKE, *Some Considerations of the Consequences of the Lowering of Interest and Raising the Value of Money*, in *Works*, 6th edition (1759), vol. II.

15. Discussed in MACPHERSON, *The Political Theory of Possessive Individualism*, pp. 222–223.

16. *Violence in America*, Report to the National Commission on the Causes and Prevention of Violence (New York: Bantam Books, 1969), p. 104.

17. MAX WEBER, *The Protestant Ethic and the Spirit of Capitalism* (New York: Charles Scribner's, 1930).
18. SIDNEY FINE, *Laissez Faire and the General-Welfare State* (Ann Arbor: University of Michigan Press, 1966), p. 46.
19. RICHARD HOFSTADTER, *Social Darwinism in American Thought* (Boston: Beacon Press, 1958), p. 66.
20. FINE, *Laissez Faire and the General-Welfare State*, p. 118.
21. RUSSELL H. CONWELL, *Acres of Diamonds* (New York: Harper & Brothers, 1915), pp. 15–25, 49–59, *passim*.
22. FINLEY PETER DUNNE, *Dissertations by Mr. Dooley* (New York: Harper & Brothers, 1906), pp. 177–82.
23. *Webster's Third International Dictionary*, 1961.
24. RICHARD HOFSTADTER, *The Age of Reform* (New York: Random House, 1955).
25. J. LAMARCK, *Flore Française* (1778) as summarized in *The Columbia-Viking Desk Encyclopedia* (New York: Viking Press, 1953), p. 532.
26. HOFSTADTER, *The Age of Reform*, p. 39.
27. Quoted in OLIVER STATLER, *Shimoda Story* (New York: Random House, 1969), p. 164.
28. *Ibid.*
29. HOFSTADTER, *The Age of Reform*; HANS KOHN, *American Nationalism* (New York: Collier Books, 1961).
30. OSCAR HANDLIN, *Race and Nationality in American Life* (Garden City, N. J.: Doubleday, 1957).
31. *Newsweek*, 74 (Oct. 6, 1969).
32. V. O. KEY, *Southern State Politics* (New York: Alfred Knopf, 1950).
33. ROBERT LANE, *Political Ideology* (New York: Free Press, 1962), p. 78.
34. For example, see OTIS DUDLEY DUNCAN, "Inheritance of Poverty or Inheritance of Race?", *On Understanding Poverty*, DANIEL P. MOYNIHAN, ed. (New York: Basic Books, 1969), pp. 85–110. See also, WILLIAM K. TABB, *The Political Economy of the Black Ghetto* (New York: W. W. Norton, 1970).
35. For Jefferson's original paragraph see CARL L. BECKER, *The Declaration of Independence* (New York: Vintage Books, 1961), pp. 212–213.
36. Article I, Sec. 2, (3).
37. Article I, Sec. 9, (1).
38. Speech in Springfield, Illinois, June 26, 1857, in JOHN G. NICOLAY & JOHN HAYS, eds., *Abraham Lincoln, Complete Works*, (New York: Century, 1890), vol. II, pp. 315–339.
39. The variety and internal inconsistency of such grounds can be seen in excerpts found in I. A. NEWBY, ed., *The Development of Segregationist Thought* (Homewood, Ill.: Dorsey Press, 1968).
40. For discussion of the stereotypes of black men prevalent in America see STERLING BROWN, *The Negro in American Fiction* (New York: Athaneum, 1937). Examples of contemporary scholarly statements that depend on inadequate sampling techniques and stereotyped thinking that considers only one possible explanation for a set of acts open to a far wider variety of explanations are DANIEL P. MOYNIHAN, *The Negro Family: The Case for National Action* (Washington, D. C.: Office of Policy Planning and Research, U. S. Department

of Labor, 1965); and ARTHUR JENSEN, "How Much Can We Boost I. Q. and Scholastic Achievement?", *Harvard Educational Review* (Winter 1968–69).

41. For a succinct chronology of Indian History see STAN STEINER, *The New Indians* (New York: Harper & Row, 1968), pp. 318–322. Hereafter cited as S. STEINER, *Indians*.

42. In 1492 the Indian population is estimated to have been 800,000 (U.S. Commission on Civil Rights Report, 1961, vol. V, p. 116). U. S. Census Reports of 1860 indicate an Indian population of 44,021; only a decade later the 1870 Reports estimated the population to be 25,731. (Compare these statistics to the extraordinary growth of the Caucasian population in both America and Europe during the same period.)

43. A sense of their experience may be gained from several works. For Mexican-Americans see SAMORA, *La Raza*; and STAN STEINER, *La Raza: The Mexican-Americans* (New York: Harper & Row, 1970), hereafter cited as S. STEINER, *Mexicans*. For the Puerto Rican experience on the mainland see PATRICIA CAYO SEXTON, *Spanish Harlem* (New York: Harper & Row, 1965); PIRI THOMAS, *Down These Mean Streets* (New York: Alfred Knopf, 1967); and OSCAR LEWIS, *La Vida* (New York: Vintage Books, 1966).

44. STATLER, *Shimodo Story*, p. 455. See also ROGER DANIELS, *The Politics of Prejudice* (New York: Athaneum, 1969).

45. This comparison is made in the excellent biography of Townsend Harris by STATLER, *Shimodo Story*.

46. STANFORD M. LYMAN, "Red Guard on Grant Avenue," *Transaction* 7 (April 1970), pp. 20–33.

47. *Ibid.*, p. 21.

48. *United States v. Wong Kim Ark*, 169 U. S. 649.

49. For a good coverage of the program see MORTON GRODZINS, *Americans Betrayed: Politics and the Japanese Evacuation* (Chicago: University of Chicago Press, 1949), and DANIELS, *The Politics of Prejudice*.

50. *The New York Times* November 22, 1969, 24:3.

51. DUNCAN, *On Understanding Poverty*, and TABB, *The Political Economy of the Black Ghetto*.

52. LANE, *Political Ideology*, p. 68.

53. ADAM WALINSKY, "Keeping the Poor in Their Place: Notes on the Importance of Being One-up" in ARTHUR B. SHOSTAK and WILLIAM GOMBERG, eds., *New Perspectives on Poverty* (Englewood Cliffs, N. J.: Prentice-Hall, 1965), pp. 159–168.

54. Reported in *Public Opinion Quarterly*, 28 (Fall 1964), 526.

55. ARTHUR B. SHOSTAK, "Birth Control and Poverty" in *New Perspectives on Poverty*, pp. 50–51.

56. Office of the President, 1967 *Report*.

57. For examples, see DAVID CAPLOVITZ, *The Poor Pay More* (New York: Free Press, 1967); JACOBUS tenBROEK, ed., *The Law of The Poor* (San Francisco: Chandler Publishing, 1966); U. S. President's Committee on Consumer Interest, *The Most For Their Money* (Washington, D. C.: U. S. Government Printing Office, 1965); ROBERT CONOT, *Rivers of Blood, Years of Darkness* (New York: Bantam Books, 1967).

58. *The New York Times*, August 12, 1969, 18:4.

48   *Poverty, Politics, and Change*

59. *Newsweek*, 74 (October 6, 1969), 45. (Note: "undecided" answers were omitted in the report of poll findings.)

60. *Ibid.*, 34.

61. *Newsweek*, 73 (June 30, 1969), 19.

62. See *Public Opinion Quarterly*, 33 (Spring 1969), 149–150; May 1968 poll reported in *Public Opinion Quarterly*, 32 (Winter 1968–69), 696–703; October 25, 1965 poll reported in *Public Opinion Quarterly*, 33 (Spring 1969), 150; poll reported in *Public Opinion Quarterly*, 33 (Spring 1969), 152.

63. For example, LEWIS KILLIAN and CHARLES GRIGGS, *Racial Crisis in America* (Englewood Cliffs, N. J.: Prentice-Hall, 1964) investigated one Florida city in which conditions seemed optimal for biracial communication, but found similar differences in perception.

64. *Report of the National Advisory Commission on Civil Disorders* (New York: Bantam Books, 1968).

65. *The New York Times*, February 23, 1969, 1:1.

66. DONALD R. MATTHEWS and JAMES W. PROTHRO, *Negroes and the New Southern Politics* (New York: Harcourt Brace Jovanovich, Inc., 1966), Figure 12–1, p. 333.

THREE

Reflection of American Values in National Policy toward the Poor

Public policy toward the poor has always borne the mark of America's adherence to the liberal tradition, with its emphasis on individualistic materialism and antagonism toward comprehensive social planning. As one study indicated, in comparison with other western democracies the United States:

. . . . is more reluctant than any rich democratic country to make a welfare effort appropriate to its affluence. Our support of national welfare programs is halting; our administration of services for the less privileged is mean. We move toward the welfare state but we do it with ill grace, carping and complaining all the way.[1]

PRIOR TO THE NEW DEAL

One consequence of adherence to natural law, then *laissez faire* liberalism during the eighteenth and nineteenth centuries was a preference for *private* and *voluntary* rather than *public* assistance to the poor. Thus, institutional charities (churches, political ward bosses, ladies societies), individual beneficence (such as Carnegie libraries) and privately sponsored Settlement Houses were the primary sources of assistance to the poor until the twentieth century.[2] Even after the more active governmental role allowed by organic liberalism had gained widespread acceptance, a substantial minority of American "conservatives" adhered to this *laissez faire* philosophy. For example, Senator Barry Goldwater articulated the philosophy in such an appealing way that a large group of Americans saw fit to make him the Republican nominee for the office of President in 1964:

Let us, then, not blunt the noble impulses of mankind by reducing charity to a mechanical operation of the federal government. . . . Let welfare be a private concern. Let it be promoted by individuals and families, by churches, private hospitals, religious service organizations, community charities and other institutions that have been established for this purpose. . . . we can shatter the collectivist's designs on individual freedom if we will impress upon the men who conduct our affairs this one truth: that the material and spiritual sides of man are intertwined; that it is impossible for the State to assume responsibility for one without intruding on the essential nature of the other; that if we take from a man the personal responsibility for caring for his material needs, we take from him also the will and the opportunity to be free.[3]

In dealing with the Depression President Herbert Hoover unwittingly assisted in making clear to a majority of Americans the necessity for a positive governmental role. Throughout his lifetime, President Hoover spoke glowingly in favor of *laissez faire.* Therefore, when faced with those difficult years he stressed *voluntary* cooperative efforts to cope with the multiple problems of finance, agriculture, business, and labor. Continuous failures slowly laid the groundwork for public acceptance of a more decisive role for the federal government.[4]

Nevertheless, the dominance of materialistic individualism in American values may still be seen in a wide variety of empirical measures of political attitudes.[5] Invariably, since the 1930s a majority of Americans have supported only those welfare policies which have approached poverty by attempting to enable *individuals* to cope more effectively with the *existing* American economic, social, and political system (old age pensions, social security, unemployment compensation, aid to education). Consistently, any attempts at a more fundamental redistribution of resources, which are based on less materialistic or individualistic philosophies, have been attacked by the majority of Americans as "radical" and "socialistic." Available data indicate that there is widespread antagonism to "sharp shifts toward general or abstract socialist principles."[6]

THE NEW DEAL AND THE DEVELOPMENT OF WELFARE

President Franklin Delano Roosevelt came not to bury capitalism but to restore it. Sharing the dominant American belief in the value of private property and free enterprise, he aimed at a return to high production, high employment and balanced government budgets, but in dealing with widespread poverty President Roosevelt inaugurated the most far-reaching set of programs in the nation's history. For example, on August 14, 1935 an omnibus Social Security Bill was enacted that made provision for a federal/state system of unemployment insurance; a federal program of old age insurance; federal grants to states for old-age assistance; aid to the blind, dependent children, maternal and child health services, and public health programs.

Despite public rhetoric antagonistic to their alleged "socialist" or "collectivist" tendencies, these programs were fully in accord with the tenets of organic liberalism. The American social and economic systems were assumed to be basically sound, merely needing to open greater employment opportunities in order for the poor to enter the work force without further help.[7] Poverty was considered a temporary condition due to unemployment, agricultural depression or the dependence of youth, or it was considered a condition due to individual problems such as blindness, or old age. Welfare was assumed to be a temporary measure which would end with rising employment and national income. Consequently, little attempt was made to coordinate programs or to consider their broader social implications. (Creeping it may have been, socialism it definitely was not.)

Once the Depression had passed, it again became difficult to induce the American people to formulate public policy for the poor. Thus, the basic policy outline for public assistance remained the same from the New Deal into the 1960s. Meanwhile, the expectation that welfare would end through rising employment and national income proved unrealistic. On the contrary, welfare rolls grew astronomically, primarily in two categories—dependent children and the aged—both unemployable. One analyst attributed this policy lag in part to innovation that had been built into the welfare policy making process.[8] They included the automated nature of Congressional action (the Social Security Act provided an open-ended, permanent authorization; nor was there an annual, or even an occasional, dispute over appropriations.), the absence of Presidential leadership, and the absence of strong interest group participation. The Act was given such loose authorization because its authors assumed that welfare would end with rising employment.

Presidents have not been forceful spokesmen for innovation since they are responsive to an electorate voting primarily for its own interests, which are not those of the poor. The poor themselves have not formed a strong interest group to pressure Congress and the President for numerous reasons: they share some of those basic individualistic assumptions underlying the act; alienation and apathy incapacitate them; and they have problems of organizing that are inherent in the logic of collective action. All of these problems will be discussed more fully in Chapter Six.

The impact on the poor of the widespread adherence to materialistic individualism and racism is most clear in the administration of these welfare programs: There the basic American equation of material possession with moral worth has been made obvious. Russell Conwell, the post Civil War Gilded Age's major apologist of the clergy, would have approved of the spirit in which our welfare programs have been administered, as they have accorded with his precept that: "It is all wrong to be poor."[9] The consequence of such an attitude has been a welfare system that is *paternalistic, punitive, and inadequate.*

The system is paternalistic in that it treats recipients as children, destroying initiative by depriving them of the ability to control their expenditures. They are told how, where, when, and for what their money should be spent. Social workers have unlimited discretionary authority over recipients' fiscal, physical, and emotional affairs. They may make inquiries at any time of day or night, and are held completely responsible for either opening or closing a case, for budgeting, and for supervising any necessary procedures.

The system is punitive because it is based on the assumption that the poor are morally unworthy. Therefore, eligibility for public assistance depends *on how great* a sacrifice the recipient is willing to make—economic need alone is *not enough* to warrant asking for relief:

There is an implicit assumption in these requirements that a really needy person will not be a newcomer, will not sin, will have nothing to hide and therefore will submit to whatever searches of his physical premises are asked of him, and will accept intrusion into his emotional privacy by the welfare agency that dispenses services along with money.[10]

Provisions under Aid to Dependent Children not only penalized stable families but also discouraged economic initiative on the part of the poor. A family could receive no payments whatsoever if a male in the household worked, no matter how low his income. Thus, a father whose job provided minimal income could economically hinder his children by keeping a job and the family intact. For example, a dishwasher who earned $60 per week and had a wife and three children could receive welfare payments of $48 per family member per month. *If he left his family,* New York City payments for a family of four in 1969 averaged $249.75 per month, or $62 per person per month, plus medical aid and other services—*and the income was tax free.*[11] To put it bluntly, the welfare system practically encouraged him to leave his family. It also dampened any economic initiative on the part of dependent children or their mothers because any income they received was automatically deducted from welfare payments. The net result was a *smaller* total income, since a job brought added expenses of carfare, meals away from home, clothing, and Social Security deductions.

THE PUNITIVE ASPECTS OF PUBLIC HOUSING

Another of the self-serving mythologies concerning the poor and welfare, which also is widely held among the American electorate, concerns public housing.

In addition to concern for welfare payments to the destitute, organic liberals recognized that man needed basic shelter and food to be free for development. As it became increasingly clear that millions of individuals could not provide these for themselves, liberals began to formulate public policy to that end. It was the 1937 Federal Housing (Wagner) Act which made the first attempt to have the national government bear acquisition and development costs of public housing. Subsequent acts broadened the scope in this area, so that by 1970 public housing assisted nearly two and a half million poor people, whose median annual family income was $2,800.[12]

This, however, was grossly inadequate to meet the need. It reached less than 10 percent for a variety of reasons.[13] Among them might be inadequate funding; the ambivalence of Congress for over a decade to commit itself to a sustained program; and the unwillingness of localities to provide such housing. For example, communities such as San Diego, California, or Des Moines, Iowa, have provided no public housing at all. Even where it was provided, it has tended to provoke high levels of antagonism from middle class groups against any plans to build low income housing on vacant land in their areas (particularly housing for nonwhites). Consequently, public housing has generally been built in poverty areas, causing severe dislocation problems for previous residents. Furthermore, for years, public housing has refused to accept troubled families as tenants, thereby excluding a large portion of the poor.[14] Even when these restrictions were softened, the most destitute were denied shelter because they lacked the money necessary to pay the minimal rent.

Not only must public housing applicants meet financial eligibility and "good behavior" requirements, they must also *maintain* the latter in order to retain their quarters. Public housing leases are usually drawn on a month-to-month basis, to facilitate eviction. In comparing these conditions with the power that welfare case workers hold over their dependents, one specialist found that: "evictions have tended to be even more arbitrary than cash relief terminations."[15] Much of this has reflected basic antagonism toward the poor, especially racial minorities. Those who administer local programs, either commissioners or directors, function as enforcers of this antagonism—commissioners are "chosen as representative of the successful business and professional leadership of the community," and directors "are more dependent on and more closely tied to the community's political and business leaders than to the public housing tenants or to a public housing administration profession."[16]

The more serious problem with public housing has been its punitive aspects which have stifled individual growth and development, thereby maintaining and perpetuating poverty. During the 1960s a large amount of literature documented this aspect of public housing.[17] A good example of such problems was recently given by anthropologist Gerald Suttles.[18] In analyzing the social patterns of a Chicago slum, he found that most blacks lived in public housing and that Italians lived in private homes. The options and social organization of the two groups was extraordinarily different as a result of this difference.

Because they lived in private homes, the Italians could work at almost anything they chose, such as taking in boarders, washing, doing handicraft or carpentry, to add to their incomes. In contrast, public housing residents were not permitted to have *any* means through which they could develop economically at home. Moreover, whenever a resident earned more than the acceptable income, he was not permitted to remain a tenant. This increased occupancy of public housing by the dependent poor, primarily by broken welfare families.

Thus, a sense of community was difficult to develop. Nor could good examples be set for children who were continuously surrounded by adults who could not earn a living wage. The Italian families, on the other hand, had become stable by raising their income levels and could remain in their neighborhoods because they owned their homes and had community ties.

Further disruption of personality development and social organization was caused by the physical set-up of public housing: groups of high-rise apartment houses on blocks devoted entirely to residential use. However, the Italians' private houses were interspersed with stores which provided congregating centers (soda fountains or candy stores for youngsters, bars for men, grocery stores and automatic laundries for women) for social organization. Empty stores could be rented for nominal fees by local groups, such as an Italian-American club, a local Democratic club (entirely Italian) or a club for *boccie* enthusiasts. Such storefront activities provided opportunities to develop a sense of community which public housing lacked entirely. All of it contributed to the differences in rates of juvenile delinquency, crime, alcoholism, drug addiction, and suicide between the public housing residents and those of low income who lived in private homes.

By the 1960s liberals recognized the fact that the program they had intended to assist individual development had failed. The Kennedy and Johnson Administrations attempted to encourage social improvement rather than the earlier brick and mortar approach by rehabilitating the poor in public housing through the provision of social services. Four "concerted service" projects were developed in St. Louis, New Haven, Miami, and Pittsburg, California, to enhance public housing tenants' ability to achieve self-help and self-support. However, they proved a failure. As one analyst wrote:

. . . Unhappily, for this goal, concerted services made no real impact; only the professionals in HUD and in HEW were committed to its achievement. The local housing authorities had a limited interest and were not willing to yield autonomy in policy, regulations, and procedures where such yielding was necessary to make services possible . . . it could not translate official local commitments of assistance into tangible, lasting support. And it could not overcome such legislative constraints as inadequate levels of income maintenance and limitations on tenure in housing projects. . . . in most jurisdictions there is still no program for dealing with the social and emotional problems of tenants that is tailored to the particular population; . . . The ambivalence between a brick and mortar activity and a social welfare activity ends in castigation from supporters of each who feel, quite properly, that the program has not made sufficient progress in either area.[19]

THE FAILURE OF URBAN RENEWAL

Nationally subsidized urban redevelopment began with Title I of the 1949 Housing Act that provided funds for bulldozing "blighted" areas (generally defined as areas where the poor or nonwhites lived) which would be sold at a low price to promoters who would redevelop the areas.[20] The resulting clearing and construction benefited the rich and badly hurt the poor. It reduced the supply of low-income housing by displacing residents in order to clear and construct projects which benefited nonresidents, such as the New York City Coliseum or other commercial and business establishments. Many critics attacked the program as illogical and impractical on the ground that it fostered the forcible displacement of citizens, destroyed a great number of low-rent homes, and cost an exhorbitant amount of the taxpayer's money.[21]

The 1954 Housing Act provided funds for more than bulldozing. It emphasized overall planning. As with low-income public housing, it remained highly controversial in local communities. Local control fostered racial and income segregation. Thus, the net impact of the program was not directly beneficial to the urban poor.[22]

INADEQUATE NATIONAL FOOD PROGRAMS

The same paternalistic, punitive, and inadequate national policies which have developed in welfare, public housing and urban renewal programs have also characterized national food programs. Not even this most basic of needs has been met for millions of Americans.

The development of food assistance programs was an indirect admission of the inadequacy of public welfare payments,[23] but it came slowly. Until 1964 only one major national program existed—the Commodity Distribution Program, established by the Agricultural Adjustment Act of 1949. This one was more concerned with aiding farmers than the poor. It was intended as a means to distribute selected farm products such as lard, flour, dried beans, and peanut butter, for which government price supports had previously been provided. It was never intended to be a complete diet, merely a supplement. Consequently, no attempt was made at nutritional balance (it was predominantly a diet of starches and fats) nor for an adequate quantity of food for subsistence.

Many obstacles related to class and racial bias prevented even this inadequate food assistance from reaching a majority of those who needed it. Local communities were unwilling to accept the program for several reasons. They were expected to provide space, facilities, and administrative salaries, all of which would cost local tax dollars which they were unwilling to spend on the "unworthy." (Table I shows the limited nature of participation.) Moreover, many local merchants feared (based on materialistic individualism) that the program would reduce their local sales.[24] Similarly, many local farmers believed that hungry people would be more willing to work in the fields when needed.[25] As a result, many rural counties discontinued the program during the harvest season to coerce the poor into harvesting crops.[26]

The difficulty that poorly educated people encountered in establishing eligibility, completing and handling forms, and coping with the administrative red tape involved were among further obstacles. In addition, recipients were required to go to food distribution centers, which were open only once a month, and carry home their entire month's supply of food at one time. Often the centers were also inconveniently located. The elderly, ill or handicapped, or those with no transportation encountered many problems in receiving their commodity surplus foods.

Consequently, as recently as 1968, more than 500 of the poorest counties in America had no food subsidies of any kind, and three quarters of their poor received no help at all from any federal assistance programs.[27] Since then, participation has rapidly increased but the program has remained so inadequate that administrators increasingly favor the food stamp program.

Between 1939 and 1943 there was a complicated experimental food stamp program whose scope was small. The present program stems from the Food Stamp Act of 1964, when the Kennedy Administration attempted to avoid the inadequacies of commodity distribution by designing a program more concerned with aid for the poor than for farmers. The food stamp program allowed locally certified low-income families and individuals to purchase books of stamps which could be redeemed in local stores for food worth far more than the regular price. The difference between the cost of the stamps and their face value varied according to family size and income.

Despite good intentions, the stamp prices were prohibitive for those in greatest need—the destitute. In any area of the country the minimum payment was $2 per person per month for $12 worth of stamps. This may sound like a modest enough sum, but a few figures bring the picture

Table 3.1

NUMBER OF SURPLUS COMMODITIES DISTRIBUTED BY COUNTIES, JULY 1969

	NUMBER OF COUNTIES DISTRIBUTING				
State[a]	20–22 Commodities[b]	17–19 Commodities[b]	14–16 Commodities[b]	11–13 Commodities[b]	8–10 Commodities[b]
Alabama	23	23	....	....	....
Arizona	....	1	10	4	....
Arkansas	....	17	....	....	....
California	23	5	1	....	....
Connecticut	4	....	....	....	....
Delaware	....	....	3	....	....
Florida	41	11	1	....	....
Georgia	9	45	23	1	....
Idaho	2	7	3	....	....
Indiana	11	27	17	8	3
Iowa	....	9	....	....	....
Kansas	5	8	1	....	....
Kentucky	15	46	....	....	....
Louisiana	2	1	11	....	....
Maine	....	11	4	....	....
Maryland	....	....	1	....	....
Massachusetts	9	7	4	1	....
Michigan	....	40	....	....	....
Minnesota	8	9	1	2	....
Mississippi	36	3	....	....	....
Missouri	12	33	18	1	....
Montana	....	....	6	3	....
Nebraska	1	....	1	....	....
Nevada	....	10	1	1	....
New Hampshire	....	6	3	1	....
New Jersey	....	7	3	1	....
New Mexico	....	10	....	....	....
New York	....	3	34	10	1
North Carolina	51	8	....	....	....
North Dakota	1	5	4	....	1
Ohio	....	4	10	2	....
Oklahoma	50	22	1	....	....
Oregon	32	2	....	....	....
Pennsylvania	....	2	7	7	....
Rhode Island	....	15	1	....	....
South Dakota	27	4	1	....	....
Tennessee	....	13	1	....	....
Texas	35	92	3	....	....
Virginia	17	22	1	....	....
Wisconsin	34	12	1	....	....
Wyoming	....	....	2	....	....

Source: *Congressional Record*, daily ed., Sept. 15, 1969, p. H7917.
a. States not listed did not have surplus commodity program.
b. A commodity group is counted if any one item in the group was distributed.

for the poor into sharper focus. If a person were to spend an average of a mere $.30 per meal, he would be spending $.90 per day, or approximately $27 dollars per month for food. Under the minimal food stamp payments, he would pay over $4 per month for $27 worth of stamps. Thus, a family of five would pay over $20 per month for the barest of subsistence diets. The fact that the money had to be paid in a lump sum (for administrative convenience) created further problems for those destitute families that could not easily accumulate $20. Of course it would have been much more convenient to pay for as many stamps as available funds could purchase but their need was never considered.

Many communities did not want the food stamp program for reasons similar to their reluctance to have the commodity distribution program—administrative costs and community hostility to the poor. In localities that provided the program many of the poor were prohibited from participating by bureaucratic red tape and rigidity. For example, if an individual missed purchasing food stamps more than two times in six months, he was required to go through the entire recertification process.[28] Those who did participate were often victimized by local merchants who raised prices for them.[29]

The degree to which the paternalistic, punitive administration and cost of the food stamp program have adversely affected the poor may be judged by the sharp drop in recipients when counties shifted from direct distribution of surplus foods to the stamp plan (both could not be provided in a county). Among all counties that shifted from surplus food to food stamps by 1968 "there was an average decline of 40 percent in persons participating."[30] The food stamp program simply failed to reach those who could not afford it. Nor was this a temporary drop due to administrative changeover, despite Department of Agriculture assurances to that effect. As recently as September 1969 a Senate committee found that:

Nationally only 21.6 percent of the poor people living in counties with food stamp programs participate in the program. . . . Only 116, or 10 percent, of all counties with food stamp programs reached 40 percent or more of their poor.[31]

In addition to the food stamp program, two further federally funded food assistance programs were established in the 1960s. They were designed to meet the nutritional needs of school children. The National School Lunch Act of 1964 provided low cost hot lunches, but many poor families could not afford the cost of $1.25 per week per child, and schools in poor neighborhoods lacked the facilities for the program. The Child Nutrition Act of 1966, which provided a school milk program, had similar problems. Thus middle-class children have benefited more from the school lunch and milk programs than have poor children.

Eventually, the inadequacy of food assistance programs could no longer be ignored. Public awareness of the problems was aided by a series of reports in 1967 and 1968 which left no doubt that starvation and malnutrition afflicted *millions* of Americans, and that government programs were seriously inadequate to meet existing need.

In 1967 several government studies documented inadequacies in the food stamp program in Mississippi. These were given wide media coverage when a Senate committee, which included Robert and Edward Kennedy, found acute hunger and malnutrition among families in the Delta area. A report by six physicians for the Field Foundation concluded that children in rural Mississippi:

. . . are suffering from hunger and disease and directly or indirectly they are dying from them—which is exactly what "starvation" means. . . . Their parents may be declared ineligible for commodities, ineligible for the food stamp program, even though they have literally nothing.[32]

In 1968 an independent citizen's board of inquiry into hunger and malnutrition in the United States published *Hunger, U.S.A.*, which documented hunger and malnutrition "affecting ten million Americans" throughout the nation, and vigorously attacked the commodity distribution and food stamp programs.[33] Five national women's organizations with some religious connections published *Their Daily Bread*, a study which found that about four million needy children in public elementary and secondary schools throughout the nation did not receive lunch.[34] Shortly thereafter, the Columbia Broadcasting Company criticized the Department of Agriculture in a two part report on "Hunger in America." In June the Poor People's Campaign made Agriculture Department policy the focal point of its attack. Further congressional investigation followed.

This crescendo of criticism resulted in some changes in the food stamp and commodity distribution programs. For those destitute who wished to purchase food stamps, lower levels of expenditure were required, as shown in Table 2. Thus, a family of five with a monthly income under $19.99 would only need $2.50 to purchase $126 worth of food stamps. While this greatly improved the food stamp program, the fact that there were so many large families with so little income was indicative of the inadequacy of the welfare program in reaching those who were destitute.

The commodity distribution program was improved through the provision of a better balanced diet. However, this did not end bureaucratic rigidity. Perhaps the best symbol of American attitudes in admin-

Table 3.2.

COST OF FOOD STAMPS, BASED ON MONTHLY INCOME, 1970

In dollars

	COST OF STAMPS							
MONTHLY NET INCOME	1 person, $28 value	2 persons, $56 value	3 persons, $84 value	4 persons, $106 value	5 persons, $126 value	6 persons, $144 value	7 persons, $162 value	8 persons, $180 value
0 to 19.99	0.50	1.00	1.50	2.00	2.50	3.00	3.00	3.00
20 to 29.99	1.00	1.00	1.50	2.00	2.50	3.00	3.00	3.00
30 to 39.99	4.00	4.00	4.00	4.00	5.00	5.00	5.00	5.00
40 to 49.99	6.00	7.00	7.00	7.00	8.00	8.00	8.00	9.00
50 to 59.99	8.00	10.00	10.00	10.00	11.00	11.00	12.00	12.00
60 to 69.99	10.00	12.00	13.00	13.00	14.00	14.00	15.00	16.00
70 to 79.99	12.00	15.00	16.00	16.00	17.00	18.00	18.00	19.00
80 to 89.99	14.00	18.00	19.00	19.00	20.00	21.00	22.00	22.00
90 to 99.99	16.00	21.00	21.00	22.00	23.00	24.00	25.00	26.00
100 to 109.99	18.00	23.00	24.00	25.00	26.00	27.00	28.00	29.00
110 to 119.99	.....	26.00	27.00	28.00	29.00	31.00	32.00	33.00
120 to 129.99	.....	29.00	30.00	31.00	33.00	34.00	35.00	36.00
130 to 139.99	.....	31.00	33.00	34.00	36.00	37.00	38.00	40.00
140 to 149.99	.....	34.00	36.00	37.00	39.00	40.00	42.00	44.00
150 to 169.99	.....	36.00	40.00	42.00	44.00	46.00	48.00	50.00
170 to 189.99	.....	.....	46.00	48.00	50.00	52.00	54.00	56.00
190 to 209.99	.....	.....	52.00	54.00	56.00	58.00	60.00	62.00

Table 3.2. (continued)

COST OF FOOD STAMPS, BASED ON MONTHLY INCOME, 1970

MONTHLY NET INCOME	COST OF STAMPS							
	1 person, $28 value	2 persons, $56 value	3 persons, $84 value	4 persons, $106 value	5 persons, $126 value	6 persons, $144 value	7 persons, $162 value	8 persons, $180 value
210 to 229.99	....	....	58.00	60.00	62.00	64.00	66.00	68.00
230 to 249.99	....	....	64.00	66.00	68.00	70.00	72.00	74.00
250 to 269.99	....	....	66.00	72.00	74.00	76.00	78.00	80.00
270 to 289.99	....	....	....	72.00	80.00	82.00	84.00	86.00
290 to 309.99	....	....	....	76.00	84.00	88.00	90.00	92.00
310 to 329.99	....	....	....	80.00	84.00	88.00	96.00	98.00
330 to 359.99	....	....	....	80.00	88.00	92.00	100.00	102.00
360 to 389.99	....	....	....	82.00	92.00	96.00	104.00	106.00
390 to 419.99	....	....	....	....	96.00	100.00	108.00	110.00
420 to 449.99	....	....	....	....	98.00	104.00	112.00	114.00
450 to 479.99	....	....	....	....	....	108.00	116.00	118.00
480 to 509.99	....	....	....	....	....	112.00	120.00	122.00
510 to 539.99	....	....	....	....	....	....	124.00	126.00
540 to 569.99	....	....	....	....	....	....	126.00	130.00
570 to 599.99	....	....	....	....	....	....	....	134.00
600 to 629.99	....	....	....	....	....	....	....	138.00
630 to 659.99	....	....	....	....	....	....	....	140.00

Source: U.S. Department of Agriculture, press release 3837–69.

61

istering the "improved" commodity distribution program might be a five pound block of cheese. To those Americans who received federal food distribution, two pounds of cheese were allotted monthly in 1970. The cheese, however, was sent to local distributors in wrapped five pound blocks, presumably for the convenience of shippers or packagers (for a while it had been packed in two pound pieces). By law, distributors were not allowed to unwrap and divide the blocks. Consequently, a single recipient received one five pound block of cheese to last two months, then one five pound block of cheese to last three months. To those who administered the program, this tidily averaged out to two pounds of cheese per person per month over a five month period. To the recipients it meant no dairy products for a month or more at a time, since homes without electricity or other refrigeration were unable to preserve a block of cheese that had been unwrapped over the stipulated three month period. Similar difficulties arose with the packaging and distribution of other products.[35] It was apparently an article of administrative faith that poverty programs should consider the convenience of any and all but the poor.

THE WAR ON POVERTY

The same inadequacies which prompted liberals to develop the housing and food programs also prompted them to consider the nation's welfare policies. Unfortunately, despite a promising start, the resulting War on Poverty foundered on the familiar rocks of widespread public hostility to the poor, especially the nonwhite poor.[36]

The primary legacy of the Kennedy years to the War on Poverty was not programs such as the Area Redevelopment Act of 1961 and the Manpower Training Act of 1962. Rather, it was personnel. For the first time since the heady days of the New Deal, the President attracted as his personal advisors and top administrators an unusually large group of innovative, creative individuals who chose to use their capacities for government service rather than private enterprise or scholarship. The aura of an active government dedicated to freeing individuals for growth and development (in contrast to the inactive Eisenhower years) was particularly attractive to organic liberals. They came to Washington in numbers from major universities, foundations, private organizations, and law firms. The problems of racial minorities, the poor, and the young were of particular concern to these men, who stayed with Johnson during the transition period after Kennedy's assassination. These problems were highlighted by several factors in the early 1960s, including the publication of two influential books and recognition of a major population change.

In 1961 Oscar Lewis had published *The Children of Sanchez* which popularized in academic circles, the concept of the "culture of poverty."

A year later Michael Harrington had published *The Other America*, a book about the nature and extent of American poverty. Theodore Sorensen read about the latter in a review by Dwight MacDonald in *The New Yorker* early in 1963, and a copy was given to President Kennedy by his chairman of the Council of Economic Advisers.[37] These and similar publications spurred the Kennedy advisers to further thought.

By 1960, a major shift of black population from the rural South to urban areas resulted in substantial black populations in the slums of Northern cities whose frustrations and anger were mounting. They erupted in violent riots for several years in the mid-1960s.

Thus, prior to President Johnson's administration, the men who would eventually be his top advisers for a few years had been made aware of the poverty problem. Several groups and individuals had already begun formulating proposals to cope with it. For example, in September, 1963 President Kennedy appointed a Cabinet level Task Force on Manpower and Conservation. Shortly after his assassination, the Task Force reported that on the basis of physical and psychological examinations one third of the nation's youth would be found unqualified for military service, primarily due to poverty.[38] Meanwhile, research and the growing civil rights movement had documented the degree to which racial discrimination was responsible for much poverty.

All of these factors provided the background for the "war" that President Lyndon Johnson called on poverty in January 1964. It was intended to be a "total war on poverty" to eliminate poverty and restructure society by giving the poor a chance to design and administer antipoverty programs. In both its avowed intent to involve the poor in the decisions which affected their lives and in its lack of racial bias, it marked a radical departure from previous public policy toward the poor.

This innovation was possible because the Economic Opportunity Act of 1964, which provided its basic legislative authorization, was developed very quickly (between January and March) by a comparatively small body of men within the Executive branch who shared the same concerns, and who were Kennedy advisers remaining in the Johnson Administration.[39] Congress was merely asked to ratify the bill, which it did quickly (Summer 1964) and with relatively little change in the Executive proposal.

The most radical innovation of the Economic Opportunity Act was the concept embodied in Section 202 (a) (3) of "maximum feasible participation of the poor"—the basis for the Community Action Program. Analysis of its legislative history indicates that the provision became part of the law because it remained unnoticed in the EOA until after passage. It was inserted in the Administration's draft of the bill by a small staff group in the Bureau of the Budget and the Justice Department, after very little discussion, and received little attention in the bill's passage on Capitol Hill.[40] In fact, the legislative history of the entire EOA clearly states that it was not the reflection of a major change in American values, but of those of a particular small group of Presidential advisers. Once its provisions were applied the EOA raised a storm of controversy.

The Office of Economic Opportunity was established as part of the Executive Office of the President with broad coordinating responsibilities for poverty programs, such as organizing community action, job training, educational programs, legal aid, medical programs, and aid for migrant laborers. In order to reach the "inner city" poor and other disadvantaged groups the OEO often attempted to bypass state and local governments. Its vague mandate also brought it into conflict with established bureaucratic centers in federal departments, such as Agriculture, Health, Education and Welfare, Labor or Interior. Thus, it initially antagonized many established holders of political power, especially mayors of large cities, who were most directly affected by community action programs. Moreover, the public came to perceive the programs as having been designed primarily for ghetto residents. Consequently, in addition to general public hostility to the poor, widespread racism provided further impetus for attack on the programs. As reflected by the public opinion polls discussed in Chapter 2, the fact that blacks received *any* assistance made many whites (particularly working-class whites) erroneously believe that blacks were being given more opportunities than whites to achieve goals which Americans valued.

In short, the War on Poverty upset such a large body of Americans that it provided the incentive needed for eventual destruction or dilution of most of the programs through outright termination, inadequate funding, or pressure to change some to the point that they no longer filled the purposes for which they had been established. In fact, the degree to which individual provisions of the War on Poverty were altered under public attack correlated directly with the degree to which these same provisions attacked American values.

Project Head Start was least threatening, therefore least threatened. Embattled from the start, however, were the Master Teacher Program, which provided incentives for more competent teachers to work with the poor, the Rent Subsidy Program, which assisted ghetto residents in obtaining housing outside slum areas, and the Community Action Program.

The idea of giving people a voice in the programs which would affect their lives was the basis for the Community Action Program. It became the most controversial aspect of the "War," because it undercut the paternalistic, punitive, and racist assumptions of previous welfare programs. Funding was never equal to the task and leadership of programs was undercoordinated and weak.[41] By 1965, the intention that the poor would *plan* community programs was lessened to their *carrying out* those programs planned by "experts."[42] Increasingly, in many communities the poor were not given that much authority although there were some marked successes.

As the costs of the Vietnamese War made budget cuts necessary in domestic programs, Congress increasingly opposed appropriations for the War on Poverty. Whenever budgets have had to be tightened, poverty programs have traditionally been cut first. As the economic recession of the late 1960s and early 1970s deepened, both the Johnson and Nixon administrations and state and local governments followed this pattern.

Even as apparently successful a program as Project Head Start was administered in a manner calculated to produce a maximum of publicity but a minimum of institutional change, "because it offered a day care center with "little more than milk, cookies, games, and affection" rather than a curriculum which taught specific skills and concepts necessary for poor children to perform well in school.[43] While the medical care and food provided by the program were valuable, it did not approach its intention of preparing "the whole child for life." The Nixon Administration cut funds significantly for this least offensive of all the poverty programs.

Similarly, the Job Training program did not live up to its plans[44] because it was inadequately financed, local programs did not necessarily train the poor for jobs in expanding industries, nor could jobs be found for graduates. The problem of employment among the hard-core poor proved particularly unyielding. Even in periods of full employment, according to the government, large numbers could find no jobs (Appalachian miners).

The War on Poverty did receive a great deal of publicity during the Johnson Administration but by 1970 analysts agreed that: "Most poor people have had no contact with it, except perhaps to hear the promises of a better life to come."[45] It certainly did not wage a "total war on poverty," as originally intended, which would eliminate poverty entirely. Nor did it even approach the restructuring of society.

MODEL CITIES

The problems that these programs faced with inadequate funding and general pressures which led to program dilution were also inherent in the Model Cities experiment. As liberals increasingly criticized the urban renewal program, the growing frustrations and anger of urban blacks erupted in ghetto riots throughout the nation. This provided the impetus for reevaluation of public policy which resulted in the Demonstration Cities and Metropolitan Development Act of 1966 and which initiated the Model Cities experiment. The program attempted to find the uneasy balance between community groups (primarily black), which demanded community participation, and existing bureaucracies and elected officials, who wanted no further experiments such as the Community Action Program.[46] This program was supposed to concentrate resources in a defined target neighborhood in a limited number of cities. A Community Development Agency, directly related to both the Mayor's office and the neighborhood community, was responsible for the planning.

The experiment aimed to avoid lack of coordinated planning, a major weakness of the War on Poverty. The national Model Cities Administration was to supply funds for the planning effort, and supplemental funds for the resulting five-year plan. It also was to coordinate planning for the bulk of financing which would come from previous programs and agencies that were still functioning.

In the initial planning stage the Task Force appointed by President Johnson to draft the proposal decided that, although racial integration and citizen participation were desirable goals, they would have to be minimized, to facilitate Congressional passage.[47] Their judgment proved correct, for in the struggle to obtain Congressional passage by even a narrow margin, racial integration and citizen participation were further diminished.[48] Supplemental funding also was cut from five to two years. Furthermore, the force and intensity of the program were substantially diluted by the necessity of vastly increasing the number of Model City projects in order to gain sufficient support for Congressional passage. Unlike the EOA, this legislation received detailed Congressional scrutiny, and the price of passage was high.

In administering the program, during the Johnson administration, the Model Cities staff was divided between those who wished to strengthen community participation and those who wanted to work through City Hall. The Nixon administration, however, firmly disapproved of community involvement, as the Secretary of Housing and Urban Development, George Romney, announced that the Model Cities program was intended to be and would remain a local government function centered around the Mayor's office: ". . . . local government officials must exercise final control and responsibility for the content and administration. . . ."[49] Although it was not politically feasible to ignore well organized citizen groups, the Romney directive discouraged any local Community Development Agency from new or further organization. These shifts of emphasis about citizen participation generated confusion and bitterness among many participants in the Model Cities process.[50]

The coordination that Model Cities could achieve was seriously limited by its modest financial resources. Most national agencies contributed, but grudgingly, and those supplemental funds which were available to the program had to be spread too thinly to effect substantial control.[51] It was undercut further by the Nixon administration which placed far less emphasis on cities than had its predecessor, and extensively limited funds.[52] Thus, even as imaginative a program as Model Cities has tended to be grossly inadequate in financing and in the opportunities it provided for participation by the poor.

THE NIXON APPROACH

These recurrent problems of American public policy toward the poor were not changed by the Nixon administration, whose most innovative proposal involved a new approach to welfare problems of families with children. On August 11, 1969, President Nixon proposed that a Family Assistance Plan be enacted with a national standard for minimum welfare payments to families and a definition of basic eligibility. It would enable the poor to have a guaranteed basic annual minimum income with a work incentive system which would allow those receiving relief to keep a portion of their earnings. Thus, the working poor could keep the first $60 of all monthly earnings plus half of all income beyond that amount.

While this appeared to be a major change, the plan was couched in language that embodied all the assumptions underlying previous welfare policies, and had provisions which reflected them more fully.[53] Significantly, it was one of the weakest of the many plans which were being proposed by groups in and out of the government to deal with the obvious failure of the welfare system. Numerous alternative plans with broader coverage had been suggested at the same time but President Nixon chose the one with the narrowest coverage (only families with children), weakest structure, and lowest support levels ($1,600 for a family of four).

The paternalistic and punitive phases of the new plan were based on the familiar assumption that poverty was the poor's responsibility and that by changing the poor themselves poverty would end. The plan was largely the responsibility of Daniel P. Moynihan, based on his concept of a "culture of poverty." Every physically able adult family member, except the mothers of pre-school children, or those needed to care for the ill or handicapped, would be required to enter a work training class or accept a "suitable" job to remain eligible for assistance. The widest discretion concerning the "suitability" of the job, or the appropriate subject matter for work training programs, would be allowed state and local administrators because there were no specific minimum standards for either the types of jobs or wages to be offered. From their previous experience, many spokesmen for these groups anticipated highly discriminating and punitive administration of the program.[54] Further, it was only a partial means of dealing with poverty, for, as the government estimated, out of the five million family heads who were covered, only one half would be affected,[55] and the program did not attempt to cope with the poor persons who were not attached to families with children. The program also ignored the economic realities of a job market in which three problems seemed particularly significant: 1) the lack of child-care centers would prevent mothers from taking jobs; 2) newly trained welfare recipients would not be able to find work because there was a scarcity of jobs for those already trained and/or experienced; 3) increasingly, the available jobs required extensive education which exceeded the scope and intention of the Nixon proposal.

Such criticism may remain speculative, however, as the inadequacies of the Nixon Family Assistance Program may never be tested or put into practice. In 1970, when the bill ran into legislative difficulties, President Nixon made little effort to press Congress for enactment, despite warnings by legislative supporters and his major advisers that without his firm initiative it would not be enacted.[56] Consequently, Congress failed to pass his program.

The President's lack of enthusiasm in the interests of the poor and the War on Poverty was further demonstrated when he cut funds for the OEO, Head Start, and Neighborhood Youth Corps and closed a large number of Job Corps centers.[57] In addition, Nixon's Director of the OEO, Donald Rumsfeld, fired VISTA activists who had been successful in organizing poor community groups.[58] He also discharged Terry Lenzer, head of the Legal Services program of the OEO, and his deputy, Frank N. Jones, whose prosecution of test cases, which challenged state and local government practices and laws relating to the poor had made many potent political enemies.[59] Lenzer and Jones had actively extended the legal services program of the antipoverty agency; their dismissal was widely believed to have represented the Nixon Administration's class bias against the poor (and hearty adherence to the principles of materialistic individualism).

CONCLUSION

Poverty became the subject of national public policy relatively late in America's history, but since the nineteen thirties a number of programs have been enacted to deal with aspects of the problem. Despite the varied aspects of poverty with which they have dealt, these programs have tended to be inadequate, paternalistic, and punitive. There also appears to have been a general bias in the way in which most of these programs have been designed, with the result that they have often tended to benefit the well-to-do more than the poor. Consequently, national policies have tended to maintain and perpetuate American poverty.

Notes

1. HAROLD L. WILENSKY and CHARLES N. LEBEAUX, *Industrial Society and Social Welfare* (New York: Free Press, 1965), p. xvii.

2. CLARKE A. CHAMBERS, *Seedtime of Reform* (Ann Arbor, Mich.: University of Michigan Press, 1967).

3. BARRY GOLDWATER, *The Conscience of a Conservative* (New York: MacFadden Publications, 1964), pp. 76–77.

4. ALBERT U. ROMASCO, *The Poverty of Abundance* (New York: Oxford University Press, 1965).

5. For a compilation and evaluation of most available empirical research on American political attitudes see JOHN P. ROBINSON, JERROLD G. RUSK, and KENDRA B. MEAD, *Measures of Political Attitudes* (Ann Arbor, Mich.: Survey Research Center Institute for Social Research, 1968).

6. *Ibid.*, p. 35.

7. THOMAS GLADWIN, *Poverty U.S.A.* (Boston: Little Brown, 1967), p. 28.

8. GILBERT Y. STEINER, *Social Insecurity* (Chicago. Rand McNally, 1066) chap. 2.

9. CONWELL, *Acres of Diamonds*, pp. 15–25, 49–59.

10. G. STEINER, *Social Insecurity*, p. 108.

11. Statistics from *The New York Times*, August 12, 1969, 18:4.

12. GILBERT Y. STEINER, *The State of Welfare* (Washington, D.C.: Brookings Institution, 1971), p. 122.

13. *Ibid.*, p. 127.

14. *Ibid.*, p. 125

15. *Ibid.*, p. 175.

16. *Ibid.*, p. 185.

17. For example, see JANE JACOBS, *The Death and Life of Great American Cities* (New York: Random House, 1961); DANIEL M. WILNER, *et al.*, *The Housing Environment and Family Life* (Baltimore: Johns Hopkins Press, 1962); "A Report on Urban Renewal in the United States," *The Urban Condition*, LEONARD DAHL, ed. (New York: Basic Books, 1963); "The Limitations of Public Housing," *Journal of the American Institute of Planners*, vol. 29 (November 1963),

70 *Poverty, Politics, and Change*

p. 284; RICHARD T. WHALEN, *A City Destroying Itself* (New York: William Morrow, 1965); JOSEPH LYFORD, *The Airtight Cage* (New York: Harper & Row, 1966); ALVIN L. SCHORR, *Slums and Social Insecurity* (U.S. Department of Health, Education and Welfare, Washington, D.C., 1966); LAWRENCE M. FRIEDMAN, *Government and Slum Housing* (Chicago: Rand McNally, 1968); LEONARD FREEDMAN, *Public Housing* (New York: Holt, Rinehart and Winston, 1969).

18. GERALD D. SUTTLES, *The Social Order of the Slum* (Chicago: University of Chicago Press, 1968).

19. G. STEINER, *The State of Welfare*, pp. 151–153.

20. For a discussion of the urban renewal problem see MARTIN ANDERSON, *The Federal Bulldozer* (New York: McGraw Hill, 1964); JEWEL BELLUSH and MURRAY HAUSKNECHT, eds., *Urban Renewal: People, Politics and Planning* (Garden City, N. Y.: Doubleday, 1967); JAMES Q. WILSON, ed., *Urban Renewal: The Record and the Controversy* (Cambridge, Mass.: M.I.T. Press, 1967).

21. For example, see ANDERSON, *The Federal Bulldozer*, p. xix.

22. FRIEDMAN, *Government and Slum Housing*.

23. G. STEINER, *The State of Welfare*, p. 191.

24. ROGER L. HURLEY, *Poverty and Mental Retardation: A Causal Relationship* (New York: Random House, 1969).

25. MOORE, *The Slaves We Rent*.

26. Citizen's Board of Inquiry into Hunger and Malnutrition in the U.S., *Hunger, U.S.A.* (Boston: Beacon Press, 1968).

27. HURLEY, *Poverty and Mental Retardation: A Causal Relationship*.

28. Hearing before a subcommittee of the Senate Committee on Agriculture and Forestry, *Food Stamp Appropriations Authorization*, 90th Congress, First Session, 1967, p. 54.

29. *Hunger, U.S.A.*

30. G. STEINER, *The State of Welfare*, p. 213.

31. Prepared by the Senate Select Committee on Nutrition and Human Needs, *Poverty, Malnutrition, and Federal Food Assistance Programs: A Statistical Summary*, 91st Congress, First session, 1969, p. 29.

32. *Poverty: Hunger and Federal Food Programs* (New York: Field Foundation, 1967), p. 60.

33. *Hunger, U.S.A.*

34. A study of the National School Lunch Program by the Committee on School Lunch Participation under the direction of FLORENCE ROBIN, *Their Daily Bread* (Atlanta: McNelley-Rudd Printing Service, n.d.).

35. Interview with Peter Khanbegian, Director of Food Program, Hancock County, Maine Opportunity Council, June 3, 1970.

36. For several trenchant discussions of this process see SAUL D. ALINSKY, "The War on Poverty—Political Pornography;" and JAMES RIDGEWAY, "The More Glorious War, in CHIAM ISSAC WAXMAN, ed., *Poverty: Power & Politics* (New York: Grosset & Dunlap, 1968), pp. 171–179, 202–216; SAR A. LEVITAN, *The Great Society's Poor Law* (Baltimore: Johns Hopkins Press, 1969).

37. LEVITAN, *The Great Society's Poor Law*, p. 13.

38. JOHN C. DONOVAN, *The Politics of Poverty* (New York: Pegasus, 1967), p. 26.

39. For fuller discussion of the process see *Ibid.*, chap. 2.

40. *Ibid.*

41. ARTHUR B. SHOSTAK, "Old Problems and New Agencies: How Much Change?" in WARNER BLOOMBERG and HENRY SCHMANDT, eds., *Power, Poverty and Urban Policy* (Beverly Hills, Calif.: Sage Publications, 1968); ROGER H. DAVIDSON and SAR A. LEVITAN, *Antipoverty Housekeeping* (Institute of Labor and Industrial Relations, University of Michigan and Wayne State University, 1968).

42. DONOVAN, *The Politics of Poverty*, and RALPH M. KRAMER, *Participation of the Poor* (Englewood Cliffs, N. J.: Prentice-Hall, 1969).

43. CHARLES E. SILBERMAN, "The Mixed-Up War on Poverty," in WAXMAN, *Poverty: Power & Politics*, p. 94.

44. For a fuller discussion of these problems see JOSEPH A. KERSHAW, *Government Against Poverty* (Chicago: Markham, 1970), chap 5; *Training and Jobs for the Urban Poor*, Committee for Economic Development, New York, C.E.D. (1970).

45. KERSHAW, *Government Against Poverty*, p. 161; LEVITAN, *The Great Society's Poor Law.*

46. JUDSON L. JAMES, "Federalism and the Model Cities Experiment," paper delivered at the Annual Meeting of the American Political Science Association, Los Angeles, September 8–12, 1970, p. 2.

47. NICHOLAS BLOOM, "The Demonstration Cities and Metropolitan Development Act of 1966," cited in *Ibid.*, p. 5.

48. ROBERT B. SEMPLE, JR., "Signing of Model Cities Ends Long Struggle to Keep It Alive," *The New York Times*, November 4, 1966, 1:7.

49. GEORGE ROMNEY, statement before the subcommittee on Housing of the House Committee on Banking and Currency, Washington, D. C. (May 12, 1969).

50. J. JAMES, "Federalism and the Model Cities Experiment," p. 23.

51. *Ibid.*, p. 25.

52. *Ibid.*

53. Reported in *The New York Times*, August 12, 1969, 18:3.

54. For example, see GEORGE A. WILEY, Executive Director of the National Welfare Rights Organization, "Why Welfare Won't Work," *The New Generation*, vol. 52 (Winter 1970), pp. 22–25.

55. Secretary of Labor GEORGE P. SHULTZ, "The Nixon Welfare Plan," *The New Generation*, vol. 52 (Winter 1970), p. 5.

56. Reported in *The New York Times*, May 1, 1970, 13:2; July 2, 1970, 1:3; July 9, 1970, 36:3.

57. As an economy measure, 75 Job Corps Centers were closed in 1969 alone.

58. ROBERT SHERRILL, "De-escalator of the War on Poverty," *The New York Times Magazine* (December 13, 1970), 102.

59. Discussed in *Ibid.*; JACK ROSENTHAL, "Legal Aid and Politics," *The New York Times*, November 24, 1970, 20:3.

FOUR

Reflection of American Values in Attitudes and Procedures of the Professions

The values of materialistic individualism and ethnocentrism, which have been so persistently reflected in American public policy toward the poor, have been equally reflected in the practices and procedures of those professions providing the basic educational, health, legal and welfare services on which the poor depend. Whatever may have been the class origins of these professionals (initially most were white and had middle-class backgrounds), by definition they have become members of the middle class, in attaining their professional roles. The function of most professions in all societies has entailed both conservation and transmission of the society's dominant values. (While this has been particularly true of education and law, it has also been relevant for medicine and social work.) In America, the dominant practices and procedures of these professions have reflected materialistic individualism and ethnocentrism.

This state of affairs has had a twofold significance for the poor: 1) the essential services upon which they have depended have not met their needs and 2) the impact of contacts with middle-class professionals (particularly in education) on their self-image has been psychologically crippling. These contacts have led to a negative self-image and have reinforced the alienation and apathy which have traditionally incapacitated the poor from developing their own alternative to prevailing values and policies.

A word of caution seems in order here. There is no intention of categorizing all individual professionals. Various professional organized groups and individuals have tried valiantly to assist the poor; many have recognized the multiple problems and have attempted to reform their own professions. They have, however, remained a minority. Consequently, the following pages concentrate on the *dominant* attitudes and procedures of each profession toward the poor.

MEDICINE

Summarizing the health problems of the poor, the Dean of Harvard Medical School recently wrote that:

In every area that relates to health the poor are deprived. They are less well informed than other social groups about general health matters, they depend more upon lay advice, and they are relatively powerless in the medical care system. That part of the population who can afford the price can purchase directly, or indirectly via insurance, fee-for-service medicine and can exert some influence over the system, but the poor are dependent to a significant degree on "clinic medicine" which tends to be fragmented, dehumanized, and lacking in continuity. Not only does the poverty group receive a different quality of care for physical illness but even the stresses and anxieties associated with illness are treated differentially according to social class. Medical care is a middle-class commodity, and the poor are discriminated against medically just as they are educationally.[1]

The poor suffer severely from nearly every physical and emotional illness known. The causal relationship between poverty and ill health has been documented in myriad studies. To point out only a few made within the past decade, in the following areas, an inverse relation has been found to exist between income level and:

malnutrition: which is a typical example of the impact of American values of individualistic materialism on the poor, as *Hunger U.S.A.* indicated: "The failure of federal efforts to feed the poor cannot be divorced from our nation's agricultural policy, the congressional committees that dictate that policy and the Department of Agriculture that implements it; for hunger and malnutrition in a country of abundance must be seen as consequences of a political and economic system that spends billions to remove food from the market, to limit production, to retire land from production, to guarantee and sustain profits for the producer."[2]

    prenatal death (particularly from causes directly related to malnutrition);[3]

    infant mortality (particularly from those weaknesses and malformations directly related to malnutrition);[4]

    communicable diseases, such as tuberculosis or venereal disease, and illnesses related to generally weakened physical organs or organic dysfunction, such as rheumatic fever, heart disease, cardiovascular disorders, visual impairment or cancer;[5]

    problems particularly (though not exclusively) connected with the aged such as rheumatism and arthritis;[6]

    physical disability (particularly relatively severe chronic illness leading to limitation of activity);[7]

multiple disabilities, disorders and diseases (particularly increasing with age);[8]
dental caries and periodontal disease;[9]
mental illness.[10]

Summarizing the health problems of the poor, one doctor wrote that: "There may be some rare condition that the poor resist better than the rich, but we have not yet found it."[11] (Gout, perhaps?)

The health problems among some groups of the poor have severely affected their life span. For example, infant mortality among Indians is sixty percent higher than the national average.[12] The mortality rate for most diseases, especially infectious ones, is higher for nonwhites than whites.[13] Studies of individual urban black ghettoes indicate that many diseases remain problems for blacks that have been practically eliminated for urban whites, e.g., polio or diphtheria.[14] Health problems of the poor in general are severe, but those with the most grave problems are nonwhites, the aged and migrants.

Particularly debilitating is the tendency for several illnesses to occur simultaneously. This is called the "clustering principle." Multiple physical disorders—neglected or poorly cared for—create a complex of degenerative diseases, which strikes by about the age of forty-five. This has been described as "the avalanche phenomenon."[15] The aged poor, then, have many particularly severe chronic health problems.

Why do the poor have greater health needs and problems than any other group? Because their problems—cyclical in nature—are both a *cause* and a *reflection* of their low status. Personal characteristics, for example, such as apathy, fatalism, hostility to middle-class white professionals and fear of hospitals, which have developed through the experience of poverty, have contributed substantially to their disabilities.[16] However, their problems have been vastly enhanced by the values of American health professionals as expressed in the organization of health services.

THE NATURE OF HEALTH SERVICES IN THE U.S.

Although the United States has the world's most advanced medical knowledge and technology, it has inherent deficiencies which compromise the accessibility and quality of medical care for *all* Americans.[17] These include:

maldistribution of medical services are such that large areas of the country lack minimal care, whereas health services cluster in others;
the pervasive trend of the last generation toward medical specialization that has resulted in a lack of general practitioners to cope with initial or immediate health needs and to maintain a continuity of overall health care;

predominance of solo medical practice which is both inefficient and costly;

uncoordinated hospitals, each of which functions independently in terms of services offered which leads to duplication of many services and omission of others, and admissions policies that add to the inefficiency and cost of medical care;

the tremendous cost of health care in America.

All of these problems stem from the pervasive commitment of American medicine to materialistic individualism. American medicine is a business, therefore most services are sold and distributed according to the supply and demand of the economy rather than on the basis of medical needs. Thus, health professionals—doctors, dentists, psychiatrists and nurses—are also small businessmen and women, who are obviously engaged and implicated in the business of American medicine.

IMPLICATIONS FOR THE POOR

Naturally, then, the increases in the cost of medicine limit the capacity of the poor to provide for their health needs. This business philosophy is clearly articulated by the leading spokesmen for organized medicine in this country, who staunchly maintain that medical care is a *privilege* rather than a right. Organized dentistry, psychiatry and nursing have made statements similar to those of a recent president of the American Medical Association, Dr. Milford Rouse, who has asserted that nonprofit medicine would be a threat to capitalism and "the American way of life."[18]

To protect these rights, organized medicine has lobbied actively to support candidates who favor their viewpoint, and to oppose passage of bills which would provide wider distribution of health services for the needy. For example, the American Medical Association spent millions to conduct a remarkably effective delaying action against Medicare and Medicaid, from 1948, when Medicare was proposed by President Truman to its eventual passage with Medicaid under President Johnson.[19] After passage, the AMA continued campaigning to limit the effect of Medicare and Medicaid provisions.[20] American medicine has also restricted access to the field, limiting the number of accredited practitioners, and resulting in a good market for health professionals, but in an inadequate number to meet even the health needs of middle-class America.

Due to its middle-class orientation, medical training and research has had significant "blind spots." For example, the recent major study of hunger and malnutrition in America found a "shocking absence of knowledge in this country about the extent and severity of malnutrition." It was attributed in part to lack of concern for researching the problem and the absence in medical education of any training which would enable medical practitioners to recognize the symptoms.[21] There have been similar blind spots, such as the lack of records kept regarding the incidence of worms and parasitic diseases among people (as opposed to the accurate records kept regarding these diseases among commercially grown cattle) the incidence of rat bites, or types of mental health problems characteristic of the poor.

Neither does medical training equip one to break through the language barriers that exist between poor people and middle-class professionals, nor to cope with the pervasive racism evidenced on the individual and institutional levels.[22] Medical practice emphasizes in-patient treatment which requires hospitalization. While a hospitalized mother or wage earner is a problem for all classes, for the poor the burden is magnified because of their marginal existence and lack of alternatives to fill these roles. Similarly, the increasingly large, impersonal, bureaucratized and inadequately staffed health institutions produce even greater psychological trauma for the poor than for other classes.[23]

PUBLIC HEALTH SERVICES AND THE POOR

While public health facilities are available, they tend to reflect the dominant equation of moral worth with material possession. Since the poor are widely considered "morally unworthy," the adequacy of these services seems irrelevant to most of those who provide them. Consequently, they are fundamentally inadequate in terms of number, distribution, and facilities; moreover, they are grossly inadequate in the manner in which they distribute services to the poor. For example, typically, they are open only during hours necessitating loss of time from work or school—particularly difficult for those with chronic problems. They tend to be located in non-poor neighborhoods, thereby maximizing transportation costs and inconvenience. They are apt to be impersonal, bureaucratic and very confusing for the poor because of their complex and contradictory eligibility requirements.[24] Their inadequacies pose particular problems for the very elderly, "tea and toast geriatrics," who are too weak to seek bureaucratic aid or cope with the system.

Public health services are not only inadequate for poor people, in general, but almost nonexistent for migrants. The fact that local communities and employers do not wish to bear the tax burden of nonresidents is of particular importance. Even when a migrant can find medical care, he frequently cannot remain in the area long enough to complete treatment. As one study indicated: "Adequate follow-up and continuity of services are aspects of civilized life the migrant simply has to do without."[25]

There were two major reasons why the Medicare program, enacted in 1966, did not significantly compensate for the deficiencies in public health services. First, the aged poor could not *afford* Medicare because the first $52 plus one-fifth of the doctor's bill, and any drugs, had to be paid by the patient. Medicare was depending on the voluntary cooperation of doctors, many of whom refused to participate for a variety of reasons. Second, Medicare assumed the state of health of the middle-class. For a person who had received adequate medical attention throughout his lifetime, hospitalization or nursing home care would probably be sufficiently short and would be covered by the program; but the aged poor have typically experienced a lifetime of poor health so there is greater likelihood of numerous and extended periods of hospitalization or nursing home care. The Medicare program, then, would only have paid for part of the required services.

The Medicaid program, passed in 1967, atempted to inaugurate a national system of basic medical care for all of the poor. Its promise was short lived, however,[26] for it depended on the willingness of individual states to provide matching funds which many were unable to meet, so they failed to provide the program or adopted it with highly restricted beneficiary categories. During the Nixon Administration growing inflation and unemployment continued to limit the tax base upon which states could draw while medical costs continued to soar. In response to these two economic problems, even states such as New York, which had initially attempted to realize the program's objectives introduced increasingly restrictive procedures to determine eligibility. Consequently, the program never had the coverage necessary to provide adequate medical services to the poor. Despite Medicare and Medicaid, health services in America have tended to be of, by, and for the middle-class.

EDUCATION

A similar entrepreneurial attitude has pervaded education more subtly. Although Americans have paid lip service to equal education for all and to education as a means for social mobility, distinct class and racial bias has actually existed. Class bias is apparent when one considers who receives education, differences in quality of education received, and the impact of teachers' attitudes toward the poor.

WHO RECEIVES EDUCATION

In considering the question of who receives education in America, distinctions should be made between elementary, secondary and higher education. For all persons until the age of 16 there are compulsory school attendance laws, but they are not invariably enforced. A variety of literature indicates the relation between income and school attendance

—70 percent of all dropouts come from families whose income is below $5,000 a year.[27] In part, increases in the dropout rate of students through the grades reflect increases in the in-school and out-of-school expenses as students advance in the "free" public school system. One study found that:

Some of the required and optional costs of keeping up were: admission fees for athletic contests, parties, dances, dramatic performances; dues for student body, class, or club memberships; fees or special assessments for homemaking, mechanical-drawing, woodworking, laboratory-science, and other courses; charges for gym clothes, lockers, athletic equipment, rooters' caps, class sweaters, rings, keys, pins; expenditures for various tag and ribbon drives, ROTC medals, school excursions, textbooks, workbooks, pens, pencils, paper, ink; subscriptions to the school yearbook, newspaper, magazine, handbook, costs of photographs for the school yearbook and for graduation, graduation announcements, diploma fees, commencement, caps and gowns.

These are simply the "in school" costs. In addition there are burdensome out-of-school expenses, such as clothes (which, as mentioned before, suddenly become the source of much social and financial concern in high school), the cost of dates, transportation by bus or car, entertaining friends or having parties at home, lunches and other meals, and other miscellaneous items.

These in-and-out-of-school expenses, when added up, are considerable enough to keep many lower-income students out of school. The mounting financial pressures in high school force many to drop out in favor of work or simply to escape from a situation where they feel "too poor in comparison with others in Class."[28]

Differentials in ability to meet these expenses are obviously class based, but social class is also related to social skills that lead to acceptance or rejection in the school environment. So children of the poor lack not only necessary clothing and cash for social affairs, homes in which to entertain friends, material possessions that form the matrix of adolescent interests in America (such as automobiles, telephones, phonographs, and transistor radios), and the leisure for extra-curricular activities if they must work, but also the verbal and social skills necessary for popularity with peers and teachers. Consequently, as they advance through the school system they experience a growing sense of social isolation and dissatisfaction. One study of high school seniors found class differences indicated in Table 4.1.[29]

These factors partially explain the increasing level of dropouts between the eighth and twelfth grades. Another factor relates to the social distinctions that are made on the basis of "ability" which is built into high school curricula that might be college preparatory, vocational, commercial or general. Schools are firm and directive in setting students on a tracking system that will mold their future options and life style. Children of the poor, particularly nonwhites, are guided away from "un-

Table 4.1

	Upper Social Status	Middle Social Status	Lower Social Status
Dissatisfaction with School:			
School is not interesting	5.0%	7.0%	12.5%
Studies are too hard	1.9%	1.3%	6.2%
Don't like my courses	3.7%	4.1%	9.8%
Difficulties in Interpersonal Relations in School:			
Not being popular	9.0%	9.4%	16.1%
Being left out of things	13.5%	11.0%	21.4%
Too few social activities	13.2%	9.1%	25.0%
Too many social activities	8.9%	4.5%	1.8%
How to make friends	10.8%	13.9%	17.9%
Difficulties in Self-expression in School Situations:			
Unable to express myself well	18.5%	23.8%	40.2%
Don't like to recite	14.0%	17.7%	19.6%
Self Criticism:			
Can't seem to concentrate	26.5%	27.2%	35.7%
Not enough time to study	15.0%	12.5%	21.4%
Afraid I'm not passing	3.1%	3.8%	8.0%

realistic" career choices, such as law or medicine, to those that seem more "realistic," along the vocational or commercial track.[30] Schools have more impact on the future of the poor because their parents are almost entirely dependent on the school system for information about vocational and educational options, whereas middle- and upper-middle-class parents basically have more knowledge and many sources of information are available to them.

The dropout problem has generally been neglected because of its complex nature, not to mention the enormous savings for the schools. Then there is the individualistic bias of the educational process which associates dropping out with student failure. Nor does the system take responsibility for such failures. Consequently, there is the prevalent belief that dropouts are not educable. The lack of attention given to compliance with compulsory attendance laws is also related.

Materialistic individualism is particularly clear with regard to two categories of the white poor: children of migrant farm workers, and children in Appalachia. There are approximately two-thirds as many children traveling with migrants as there are adult migrant workers.[31] Since the migrants pay no school taxes and are viewed as inferior by the communities through which they pass, little attempt is made to enforce school attendance laws.[32] Moreover, employers take advantage of their children during the harvest season.[33] As a result, most migrants never complete more than four years of schooling, and at least a third are functionally illiterate.[34] Thus they are unable to break the cycle of poverty. The problems that children of the poor in Appalachia have even attending school were well documented in the major study of the region, as were the limited attempts of authorities to enforce school attendance laws, and the consequent high level of illiteracy.[35]

The significance of college education has been enhanced by the "post-Industrial Revolution" that will be considered subsequently. Access to and attendance at institutions of higher learning are class-based because of their high costs which must be borne by the individual and his or her family. The 1970 Report of the Carnegie Commission on Equality in Higher Education supported the findings of earlier studies that far more students wanted to go to college than could afford to.[36] (In fact, a still earlier study of high school students found that sixty-three percent of the lowest income group *wanted* to go on to college but were financially unable to do so.)[37] The Carnegie Commission found widespread barriers to equality of education, such as the awarding of scholarships to members of higher-income groups and racial discrimination. Lower income students have been at a disadvantage for lack of even the crudest information about preparation for college: which college to choose, how to obtain and complete an application and what to do, once accepted.

QUALITY DIFFERENCES

Differences in quality of building, equipment and teachers demonstrate the degree to which class prejudice pervades American education. Schools in poor areas generally have older buildings, fewer and more outdated supplies and books, less specialized facilities such as libraries, gymnasia and cafeterias.[38] This situation is worse in areas of rural poverty, but schools tend to be much more crowded in urban poverty areas. The personnel sent to these schools is usually less qualified. This lack of experienced personnel is evidenced by an example in New York City, where one study found that twenty percent of the teachers in Spanish Harlem were substitutes, eighteen percent were probationary trainees, many more were teaching without a license and the teacher turnover rate was more than double that of the entire city.[39] Similar findings have come from other cities. For example, in poverty areas of Detroit as compared with schools in middle-class areas, three times as many emergency substitute teachers were found to be teaching in regular positions.[40]

Schools in poor areas also lack adequate supervision and teacher guidance. Thus, high teacher turnover rates reflect the result of a situation where young teachers are thrown into environments in which they lack the necessary tools of their craft, are teaching in areas outside their specialization and lack guidance from the school system.

One important reason for class-based quality differences stems from the fact that the middle class has much more ability and opportunity to influence the school system than have the poor. The professionals who plan and administer school policies as well as local school boards come overwhelmingly from upper-income groups. Income correlates with organization, participation and ability to communicate with school staff and in turn have an effect on school policies. Moreover, information about services and possible school programs correlates with income. As a result, even those programs specifically designed to help the poor are more likely to help the middle class. For example, studies have found that the free lunch and free milk programs have most often been provided in schools in middle-class areas, whereas about one half of the schools in poor sections have lacked both of these programs.[41] This is partly due to the fact that they lack the necessary facilities such as cafeterias or refrigeration, but it also reflects the fact that middle class parents are more *informed* of the existence of such programs, and thus are better equipped to *organize* to obtain them.

Another example of middle class advantage over the poor was shown in a study conducted by two private agencies of federal education funds which had been earmarked for disadvantaged children under Title I of the Elementary and Secondary Education Act of 1965, totaling $4.3 billion between 1965 and 1969. According to the study, these funds were "wasted, diverted or otherwise misused by state and local authorities" in many areas throughout the nation, while the United States Office of Education was "reluctant and timid" in using its authority to demand that the funds be used for the disadvantaged as originally intended.[42] Researchers found, in all regions of the country, that a disproportionate share of Title I money had been spent for equipment which had little relation to teaching deprived children. Other research has indicated that similar diversion of state funds occurs as well. In Appalachia, for instance, the elected school board members joined with the courthouse political machine to spend county funds and manage State Aid programs as "massive patronage dispensations," which did more to enrich the middle class than aid the poor.[43]

TEACHERS' ATTITUDES

Since much of the nation's teacher-training curricula have ignored the reality of the classroom situation, not too much effort has been directed to properly training teachers to meet the needs of lower-class children. There have been some recent changes as a result of minority group protest, but some aspects of teachers' attitudes will continue to be highly resistant to change. Teachers identify heavily with upper-income groups in terms of their opinions, aspirations and life style. This is reflected by the "reward" system in which inexperienced newcomers are placed in ghetto schools, while those who gain status move to white upper-income neighborhoods. Both the National Education Association and American Federation of Teachers have successfully fought attempts to remedy this situation by offering pay incentives to attract better qualified teachers to poor areas.

The bias of teachers is reflected in their emphasis on middle-class values which have little relation to capacity to use one's mind in a creative, analytic fashion. A case in point is the *excessive* emphasis on politeness (acquiescence and conformity), neatness, quiet, order, rote memorization, and artificial barriers to further learning that are created by the presumption that, at each grade, there is an appropriate curriculum which students in lower grades may not study, even if they are ready for it. There is a growing literature on the degree to which teachers perceive that such middle-class attributes are inherently related to mental capacity.[44] This is illustrated in the number of "gifted" children chosen for special programs. Children of the poor are rarely seen by their teachers to be "gifted," while the incidence of "gifted" children steadily increases almost geometrically with increases in income level.[45] This reflects a variety of health and language problems and unstable home life experienced by many of the poor, but it also reflects the pervasive philosophy that they are "culturally deprived,"—lacking middle-class culture, they are assumed to lack *any* culture. Yet recent studies indicate that the lack of interest shown by poor children in stories about Spot, Jane, houses with picket fences and nearby farms, stems from the irrelevance of such people and things to their life experiences, not from their inherent mental incapacity.[46]

Mental incapacity is determined in school by standardized I.Q. (intelligence quotient) tests. Actually, they reflect the middle-class bias of mental health specialists, who tend to ignore environmental causes of retardation and evaluate intellectual ability according to middle-class standards.[47] As a result, standardized I.Q. tests evaluate only a limited aspect of human intelligence: speed and accuracy, experience and vocabulary, and previous exposure to such tests (one improves with practice). More significant aspects of human intelligence are never measured, including creativity, perspective, motivation and capacity to adapt one's behavior to one's environment. (A slum child faces different demands and, therefore, has adapted his behavior in a manner different from that of a middle-class child.) Nor do standardized tests evaluate the intelligence of those lacking facility in middle-class American vocabulary, such as students whose native language is not English, and poor blacks or whites who speak a rural or ghetto dialect.

The middle-class bias of teachers has been demonstrated in numerous studies indicating that apathy and acquiescence are *expected* of students from poor families whereas active, competitive norms are *transmitted* to those who are better off. For example, one study found that teachers emphasized voting and political participation for middle-class children, but obedience and gratitude to the government for children of the poor.[48]

Individual teachers may enter the system with idealistic values, but an individual school is a small social system that has a tendency to socialize newcomers (who start on probation) to appropriate attitudes toward the students. In poor neighborhoods, particularly those dominated by minority groups, the newcomer soon learns that students are referred to as "animals," and beatings and physical brutality occur to a degree unheard of in middle-class schools. The insidious process by which an individual is coopted into acquiescence with the system was well described by a young man who experienced it:

One of the most grim things about teaching in such a school and such a system is that you do not like to be an incessant barb and irritation to everybody else, so you come under a rather strong compulsion to keep quiet. But after you have been quiet for a while there is an equally strong temptation to begin to accept the conditions of your work or of the children's plight as natural. . . .[49]

In addition, the nonwhite poor must cope with teacher racism. So much has been published about racist attitudes among American teachers toward black children that reiteration is unnecessary. Many works are listed in the footnotes.[50] A body of literature is also developing that indicates similar situations for other groups of nonwhite poor, such as Indians,[51] Mexican-Americans,[52] and Puerto Ricans.[53]

The most invidious effect of teacher racism and class prejudice is the impact that these have on intellectual growth. Children are usually responsive to the expectations of their environment, reading both the conscious and unconscious messages that adults transmit.[54] Those racist teachers who equate poverty with moral unworthiness *expect* substandard performances, so students fail because they have been "programmed" for failure. For instance, an experiment conducted in St. Louis divided students into groups of equal ability judged by objective standards. Teachers were told that one group was exceptionally gifted, and that the other was quite slow. Consequently, teachers demanded a high level of work of the "gifted" students, refusing to accept inferior work, but expected and obtained much less from the "slow" group. As a result, "gifted" students showed an increase in I.Q. and skill level scores, whereas those of the "slow" group deteriorated, indicating that a major reason pupils fall below grade level is that *substandard performance is expected of them.*[55] Other studies substantiate the fact that low teacher expectation, racial prejudice and class bias contribute to a massive deterioration in reading, arithmetic and I.Q. scores through the grades.[56] For example, when black and white children enter school there is little perceptible difference in their intelligence scores, but by the third grade those of black children begin to reflect the educational system's prejudice and low expectations. From that point on through the grades the differential grows.[57]

Another aspect of teacher expectation is its relation to health. Because many teachers assume that a slow learner is intellectually deficient, they do not initiate testing for physical disabilities which may be causing problems, such as poor vision or hearing, malformations that may require corrective surgery, metabolic or glandular disturbances or nutritional deficiencies. If such problems continue untreated they further incapacitate the child from learning, and may later cause more severe health problems.

LAW

Various studies of attitudes of the poor, particularly nonwhite poor, indicate that of all professions with which they come in contact, they view law with the greatest hostility and suspicion.[58] Analysis of the impact of the legal system's procedures and the attitudes of its personnel suggests that such a view is appropriate, as may be seen in even a brief examination of court procedures and practices, including class and racial differences in: the reasons for appearing in court; procedures related to bail and pre-trial release; procedures in civil, criminal and family cases; and access to appellate review. Furthermore, class and racial differences may be seen in the attitudes of lawyers, judges and policemen. In combination, these factors create a legal system in which American "justice" is a very expensive commodity with a definite racial bias.

COURT PROCEDURES AND PRACTICES

Initially, the poor do not go to court of their own volition, unlike many groups that enjoy more advantages and are oriented to use the courts to obtain a remedy when they feel aggrieved. Such unwillingness to seek a legal remedy is particularly significant in light of the fact (documented in a wide literature) that the poor are in greatest need of legal protection.

As consumers, for example, they are exploited by techniques such as bait advertising, misrepresentation of prices, substitution of inferior goods for those paid for, and fraud by peddlers and door to door salesmen.[59] Moreover, credit is not available from reputable sources, such as bank loans or charge accounts. Consequently, they are victimized by illegally high interest charges on heavy installment buying.[60] This ensnares them in a vicious cycle in which the fact that they are rejected as bad credit risks by legitimate merchants causes them to turn to exploitative credit merchants, and, once trapped, their credit record prohibits them from being able to get credit from legitimate merchants in the future.[61]

Similarly, in housing the poor are badly victimized. Even though they allocate a higher percentage of their income to housing, they receive lower quality per dollar spent than do the middle class. One study found that the majority of families with annual incomes under $2,000 spent thirty percent or more on rent, while only fifteen percent of the income of families earning $8,000 to $10,000 went toward rent.[62] The low quality of the housing available to poor people (falling significantly below minimum legal standards for health and safety) has been well documented, as has been the fact that the bulk of private slum housing is owned by slum property specialists who typically own no other kind. The properties are badly overpriced, under-maintained and particularly exploit minority group members who pay significantly higher rents than whites living in the same area, because racial discrimination in the housing market forces them to depend more heavily on slum properties—racism limits their housing alternatives.[63]

These factors should lead the poor to employ civil suits frequently, yet they are extremely reluctant to do so. For instance, one study found that only nine percent of those consumers who reported to the researcher that they had been cheated had sought professional help to deal with the problem.[64] This may be ascribed in part to apathy or ignorance, but it is also related to the procedures of American civil courts which place unusual burdens on the poor.

Initially, two aspects of the procedures of civil cases limit the *possibility* of the poor even using the court system as a means of defense against exploitation. First, there is no provision of a right to counsel for indigents in civil cases, for which the consequences are frequently as profound for the individual as are those of many criminal proceedings.[65] Second, unlike the practice of many other nations, in America the winning party cannot recover counsel fees from the loser.[66] Beside these obvious limitations, the poor are also inhibited from turning to the courts by procedures that are incomprehensible to the layman, especially one who is not represented by counsel, poorly educated, and consequently ineffective in communicating in legal English. A poor man's experience with civil court in a landlord/tenant dispute has been described as follows:

. . . He first receives a form piece of paper telling him to appear at the courthouse on a certain day. Assuming that he understands the import of the paper and overcomes the problems of getting to the courthouse; when he arrives, the scene is one of baffling confusion to him. No one is there to help those inexperienced in the ways of the courthouse. The tenant may eventually find his way to the clerk's office where the usual early-hour bedlam reigns. Lawyers are bustling about, calling upon harassed clerks for files and docket sheets, signing papers, and filing documents. . . . to the poor man it is incomprehensible. If the latter manages to work his way to the clerk's desk, a busy clerk may finally take notice of him and ask him what he wants. The inarticulate, confused tenant doesn't know what he wants. He starts telling about how he received a piece of paper, shuffling through his pockets for it. The clerks are not social workers and they have little patience or sympathy with the numbers of tenants who appear each day, and their attitudes unmistakably reflect this.

The tenant may finally locate the courtroom in which his case will be heard. There his suspicion that the law is for the "rich man" may be symbolically reinforced by the physical setup of the room. Typically, there is an area of several yards around the judge's bench which is marked off by a waist-high partition. Inside the partition sit the landlords, or their agents, and their lawyers. (Rarely does a tenant have a lawyer.) The landlords, their agents, and the lawyers are well-dressed in suits and ties, and there is an atmosphere of conviviality and acquaintanceship among them as they chat amiably with each other. When the judge arrives, he too is often included in the group by an exchange of friendly comments and looks of mutual understanding. Moreover, those within the partition speak a common language replete with references to technical legal terms which are wholly foreign to the tenants.

On the outside of the inner circle stretch the rows of tenants, miserably dressed and obviously poor. There is little talk as each sits quietly, some clutching in their hands a wad of dirty dollar bills. Then the ritual begins. The clerk starts by reading aloud the names of delinquent tenants. The majority of tenants do not show up, so that the names are read in rather rapid succession with the landlord or his lawyer coming in on cue after each name with the word, default, followed by the judge on cue, judgment. The monotony of the recital has some resemblance to a bingo game with an occasional response from the tenant's row, whereupon the game is halted momentarily to the sometimes obvious inconvenience of those in the inner circle. The tenant very self-consciously makes his way to the front of the room, where he starts explaining that he has had unexpected medical bills, or the house doesn't have any heat. In many courts, he is interrupted rudely and asked if he's got "the money" with him. If he does, he pays, including interest and costs, and is curtly dismissed. If he does not, the landlord may agree to give him another five days or so in which to pay, upon failure of which judgment will automatically ensue and the marshal can be sent to evict without further hearing. If he cannot promise to pay or the landlord isn't willing to wait, he is told that within a few days the marshal will appear and move all of his belongings onto the street. . . .[67]

To ease the problems faced by indigents who lack counsel, many states have established special courts (usually called "small-claims courts") for claims that do not exceed two or three hundred dollars.

Filing fees are nominal, and rules of evidence and procedures are informal. Their initial purpose, however, has been subverted, for they are primarily used by business organizations seeking to collect debts.[68] As a result, the poor are normally the defendants rather than plaintiffs in small-claims courts.

In one respect indigent defendants are more fortunate in criminal than in civil cases. A series of Supreme Court decisions during the 1960s has required that they receive "adequate representation" through court-appointed counsel, if they can obtain no other by the point at which the accused must plead to the indictment. Nevertheless, in both criminal and civil cases, the poor are disadvantaged.

There are several different systems of providing counsel for the indigent. In the federal court system and in some state court systems, counsel is selected from a list of lawyers provided by the local bar association, and receives no compensation for his services. Counsel, then, bears the financial burden of obtaining the resources adequately to defend his indigent client. This might include financing a search to locate and identify witnesses and paying for scientific aids to obtain evidence. Moreover, he must take time from his law practice to perform these services, and his time is quite valuable as is reflected by the schedule of suggested minimum fees for criminal cases compiled by local bar associations.[69]

Table 4.2

Court matters:	
Appearance and plea, felony	$250.00
(first two appearances)	
For each additional appearance	50.00
Trial per diem	250.00
Office matters:	
Office visit:	
Only service rendered under 30 minutes	10.00
Over 30 minutes	25.00 per hour
Home visit including travel time	25.00 per hour
Office work only	25.00 per hour

The costs of transcripts alone may run into hundreds or thousands of dollars.

In some state court systems, appointed counsel serve for compensation that is determined by law or by the court, and is paid from public funds. Although this eases the financial burden, he must still serve for fees below those he could obtain from private clients. Thus, for both types of court-appointed lawyers the quality of defense has tended to be inferior compared to that available for those who can pay for services.

Furthermore, court-appointed lawyers are generally young and inexperienced and consequently unable adequately to protect their clients interests.[70] These lawyers, then, are more likely to advise their clients to plead guilty for a reduced sentence than those who are privately retained:[71]

Table 4.3

PLEAS OF GUILTY BY DEFENDANTS WITH
ASSIGNED OR RETAINED COUNSEL (1962)

Place	# of cases in sample	% guilty assigned	% guilty retained
Phoenix, Ariz.	118	43	20
San Diego, Calif.	108	82	66
Boise, Idaho	29	92	71
Leavenworth, Kansas	22	83	50
Baltimore, Md.	69	44	24
St. Louis, Mo.	40	100	81
Buffalo, N.Y.	125	67	46
Newark, N.J.	129	61	43

A third system in some states to provide counsel for the indigent is that of the public defender. Counties maintain one or more salaried lawyers and a staff to devote all or most of their time to representing the indigent. In practice, this system also produces an inferior quality of defense. Because they are appointed officials, public defenders must remain attentive to the political climate. They are overburdened with cases and are not adequately compensated for extensive research. As a result, they, too, have a tendency to advise clients to plead guilty for a reduced sentence:[72]

Table 4.4

PLEAS OF GUILTY BY DEFENDANTS WITH
PUBLIC DEFENDERS OR RETAINED COUNSEL

Place	# of cases in sample	% guilty Defenders	# guilty retained
Los Angeles	244	65	47
San Francisco	141	73	56
New Haven, Conn.	48	81	77
Wash., D.C.	58	62	48
Miami	163	52	38
Queens, N.Y.	63	94	83
Boston	109	60	47
Cook County, Ill.	204	77	62

The final means through which indigent defendants in criminal cases obtain counsel is through various voluntary groups which are supported by donations and staffed by attorneys who volunteer part of their time. They share similar problems of lack of resources and a demand for services which far outweigh their ability to provide them. In 1970, New York City, for example, had a contract with the Legal Aid Society to pay a fixed amount of money to provide for lawyers and staff to represent the indigent. When the amount was divided by the number of cases handled, an average of eighteen dollars was spent by the City on each case.[73]

The poor are disadvantaged in family cases, too. Divorce proceedings are available only to those who can pay a substantial fee, as neither state-appointed attorneys nor counsel from legal aid societies will handle that type of case. Without legal divorce proceedings, custody of the children of spouses who have separated cannot be determined. Moreover, those spouses can only establish new relationships by illegal means so the children of such a union are illegitimate. When children of the poor are orphaned they do not receive the legal protections available to more advantaged children who are given a court-appointed guardian because they have an estate of their own. Guardians are rarely appointed for orphans who lack an estate.[74] Juvenile courts also have shown biases similar to those of the other court systems.[75]

Bail and pre-trial release cases have had the greatest class bias of all court procedures. As Attorney General Robert Kennedy noted:

. . . in probably no other important aspect of judicial administration are the rights and privileges of persons predicated so frankly and directly on the financial resources the individual is able to command. . . . modern bail administration places the accused with limited means at a sharp disadvantage and . . . these disadvantages proceed from the express assumptions of the system. . . .[76]

The report of a committee established by Attorney General Kennedy, to study poverty and the administration of criminal justice in the federal court system, found that the financial resources of a defendant determined whether he would receive pre-trial release. For example, the majority of defendants in federal criminal cases throughout the nation were unable to meet bail when it was set from $501 to $1500, and about one third could not meet bail set at $500 or below. Moreover, bail hearings are not usually subject to review, and they do not provide relevant factual data on the "character" or "financial ability" of defendants, which are necessary for sound bail decisions. Since counsel is rarely assigned for bail hearings, the entire proceeding depends on the discretion of a judge who must function on the basis of personal values rather than objective criteria.

Defendants who cannot post bail are detained in jail prior to their trial. Due to the extraordinary backlog of cases on almost every court docket, pre-trial detention may last for a significant period. The Attorney General's report indicated that in federal courts the average length of detention was about a month, but a large number of persons were detained from three months to a year. Delays are even greater in state courts, where delays from eighteen months to two years are not uncommon.

Pre-trial detention is especially harmful to a poor person. He must obtain evidence and track down witnesses to make an adequate defense. If he is given a lawyer, pretrial detention impedes the lawyer's contacts with his client. If he has held a job, pre-trial detention ends that income which he could use for defense and family support. The conditions of detention centers, designed for brief, temporary stays, are far more oppressive, restrictive and overcrowded than of prisons for the convicted. Some indication of how few detention centers even meet minimal standards of decency were suggested in one study:

> . . . The typical jail has a destructive effect on human character. . . . There are some 3,000 county jails in this country, and several thousand more city jails. Our Federal jail inspectors have approved 800 of these facilities for the confinement of Federal prisoners. These 800 jails by and large were not approved because they met desirable standards, but because they met the minimum standards.[77]

Furthermore, the effect upon a jury of a defendant who has been detained in jail for an extensive period may be detrimental to his case. "When a jailed defendant enters the courtroom for trial, he comes through the door leading from the lockups in the company of an officer —a point not likely to be lost on a jury."[78] After extensive detention he is likely to look worn, ill-kempt and distraught. Detention surroundings are frequently such as to change the individual's mental outlook enough to hinder his defense.

The process of appellate review functions in such a manner that it, too, is discriminatory towards the poor. Counsel and other defense services are particularly important in this process. Many indigents lose the right to appeal because of their own ignorance and reluctance or negligence on the part of assigned counsel to inform them of this right and that notice of appeal must be filed within ten days after entry of the trial judgement.

A defendant too poor to pay for trial transcripts and court costs must apply for leave to appeal *in forma pauperis* which requires multi-step screening, specifically designed to limit access to appellate courts, as reported by the Attorney General's Committee.[79]

ATTITUDES OF LAWYERS, JUDGES AND POLICEMEN

The legal profession depends upon an entrepreneurial, fee-for-services basis of financing. In 1970, lawyers' fees in America ranged from $20 per hour to well over $100 per hour. Even young inexperienced lawyers in major cities received about $35 per hour.[80] Costs were higher if a trial was required.

To maintain its economic position, the organized bar has successfully fought both legal insurance (similar to health insurance) and group legal service in which one or two lawyers handle the legal work of all persons in a specific group, such as a union.[81] (Group legal service would function for legal care as do Blue Cross and Blue Shield for health care.) Thus, attempts by lawyers to protect their economic status further disadvantage the poor.

General rudeness, prejudice, harassment and abuse experienced by indigent persons in court partially reflect the attitudes of judges in such cases. A series of studies has documented obvious racism. For example, one study on racial disparities in the length of prison sentences in the South found:[82]

The average prison sentence for white offenders in Tennessee was 12.8 years, but 22.1 years for blacks.

The racial disparity in years of sentence was under one year in Virginia, one and a half years in Alabama, two and a half years in North Carolina, six and a half years in South Carolina, seven years in Arkansas and Georgia, and nine and a third years in Tennessee.

For the same kind of crimes against the person in Arkansas, Georgia and Tennessee blacks served about seven and a half years longer than whites.

In these seven southern states the average sentence for black crimes against whites was 28 years, for whites against whites was 23.8 years, for blacks against blacks was 21.2 years, and for whites against blacks was 20.7 years.

Similar depressing patterns of racism have been pointed out in studies of enforcement of school desegregation by federal judges.[83] They reflect the usual middle-class equation of moral worth with material possession especially in bail setting and sentencing. There are, in fact, a whole series of sentences dealing with issues such as vagrancy, loitering and prostitution, which are meted out predominantly to the poor. Moreover, some are almost exclusively meted out to the poor, such as the banishment decrees of local courts that require the indigent to leave the town limits. Court abuses of migrants are particularly frequent.[84] In general, the bias of state courts of first jurisdiction protects property rights over individual rights with obvious implications for the poor in court.[85]

Reports of harassment and discrimination by policemen against the poor, especially members of minority groups are regular media features. The stereotype of the vicious Southern sheriff is part of our folk culture, but such reports from the ghettos of Los Angeles, Chicago, Detroit, Cleveland, Newark, Boston, Philadelphia, Washington, D.C. or New York are also common. Even small cities with minimal poor minority groups, such as Boise, Idaho, report such harassment.[86] Discrimination of this sort also permeates behavior of elite groups, such as the Texas Rangers. Their overt racism, intimidation and harassment of poor Mexican-Americans and blacks led the United States Commission on Civil Rights to recommend that they be disbanded.[87] The Commission found that: ". . . the elite unit has operated virtually as a private police force to protect the interest of the wealthy landholders and ranchers, that it has been used as a political weapon of intimidation by successive Governors and that it has a long tradition of hostility toward Mexican-Americans."[88]

Federal studies of police forces throughout the nation substantiate these newspaper reports. For example, in 1966 the President's Commission on Law Enforcement and Administration of Justice found that one out of ten policemen in white and black poverty areas used "improper" or "unnecessary" force,[89] and that in the slums of three Northern cities, Washington, Boston and Chicago, at least 27 percent of the police engaged in "some form of misconduct that could be classified as a felony or a misdemeanor."[90] Four major classes of police misconduct were found:

> *shakedowns* of drunks, deviants, businessmen and traffic violations;
> *theft* from burglarized establishments;
> *payoffs* to the police to return stolen property, to alter testimony at trial and to protect illegal establishments;
> *carrying extra weapons* to plant on citizens as "evidence" in case a policeman injured or killed a citizen who had not used a weapon so that the policeman could argue self-defense.

Since these acts of force were recorded by accompanying observers, it is reasonable to suspect that they seriously underrate the acts of force that would have occurred in an unobserved situation. In 1968 the Kerner Commission Report on Civil Disorders found that: "The abrasive relationship between the police and the minority communities has been a major—and explosive—source of grievance, tension and disorder."[91]

Racism and class prejudice are the underlying reasons for such conduct. Urban police forces are usually composed predominantly of second generation immigrants who have used the civil service as a means for upward social mobility.[92] They perceive the poor, particularly minority group members, as people who are also striving to attain higher status, and consequently a threat.[93] One trait found in varying degrees among policemen is authoritarianism,[94] which is expressed in terms of stereotyping, aggression and conventionality.[95] They have been found to think more in terms of the assertion of authority than of law, and to identify with the authority vested in them by virtue of their job.[96] A significant percentage are openly hostile, brusque or authoritarian in encounters with the poor,[97] and equate poverty and skin color with evil and sin.[98]

In testifying before the National Commission on the Causes and Prevention of Violence, one noted scholar on police abuse suggested that:

To the policemen all the troublemakers—the ordinary citizen, especially from a minority, who defies authority; the outcast; and the hardened criminal—are lumped together. They are all elements to be controlled. That is the policeman's conception of his job: to maintain social equilibrium at all costs. . . .

The policeman's view of his job as I have described it—punishing defiance, harassing outcasts, and otherwise generally using every means to punish "wrongdoers"—forms a fairly consistent set of values (as do the public attitudes from which it derives). Though it is not the "Rule of Law" as courts define it, it is a code. The police are adhering to their own rough rule of law; it is almost entirely substantive, and scarcely procedural at all. Under their code, any means to convict and punish a person dangerous to society—including a troublemaker as well as a man defined as criminal by the criminal law—is legitimate. Policemen will tailor their testimony in court so as to punish wrongdoing—as they see it. Public hypocrisy about the police—wanting them to enforce the informal code, while adhering to all the punctilio of due process—tends to sanction this double standard between court testimony and police practice. . . .

If the person is an outcast, like a derelict or a homosexual, or if his language is especially provocative, the police are likely to combine their sense of personal outrage and insult with their desire to punish a "criminal," by beating him up on the spot. The end result of this is likely to be the addition of charges of resisting arrest and assault to that of disorderly conduct.

The charges serve the dual purpose of covering the policeman's error in making the arrest or administering physical punishment, and punishing the "criminal" still further. The problem for the policeman is, of course, that mere defiance is not disorderly conduct or any other offense, and the "assault" charged against the citizen has frequently been administered by the police. But the policeman must cover his error, and finish his punishment. So he testifies to actions that will make out the offenses of disorderly conduct and assault —a loud, drunken argument, followed by blows. By the unwritten law of solidarity among policemen, if the arrest is made in accordance with the informal code, that is, if the citizen has defied the police before his arrest, other policemen must back up the arresting officer's story. . . .

In distorting the facts of criminal cases, either to deny procedural safeguards or to supply missing elements for offenses against the police, the police treat the courts as a sort of adjunct to the precinct. In their view, their own informal code is superior to that of the courts, and they make sure that it is their code which is enforced in the name of the Rule of Law.

Thus there is a double punishment for outcasts and those who defy authority—police violence, plus a conviction in criminal court. . . .[99]

Such behavior persists because the public *condones* it. The police function to maintain social stability and to protect basic social values. In a society whose values are materialistic individualism and racism, policemen act accordingly. American law enforcement officers are among those people who have been socialized into a society whose basic values discriminate against the poor and racial minorities, and whose job is to enforce these values.

Three distinct types of law enforcement in different communities reflect these attitudes. A "watchman" style is applied in low income areas because the police believe that these people deserve less law enforcement due to ". . . the low level of public and private morality."[100] It emphasizes mere maintenance of a semblance of order, not full enforcement of the law.[101] The poor and racial minorities thus receive less protection from the police than do more advantaged citizens, and are aware of it.[102]

A second type of law enforcement is the "legalistic" style in which commonplace misdemeanors are punished to the fullest extent of the law.[103] While there is less social and class discrimination, the poor and minority group members feel harassed because of the volume of arrests.[104]

The third is called the "service" style. Here, the police respond to all requests for maintenance of order and law enforcement, but rarely with the imposition of formal sanctions.[105] It is used in ". . . homogenous middle-class communities in which there is a high level of apparent agreement among citizens on the need for, and definition of, public order but in which there is no administrative demand for a legalistic style."[106] The middle-class community thus expects and receives courteous law enforcement.

Police bias also is responsible for arresting poor persons more often than others. Police keep arrest records but do not record final disposition. So, a black teenage boy who may have been arrested multiple times for "suspicion," but never convicted of anything, would be unable to get a job because of his lengthy "arrest record." Jobless, he would remain on the streets to encounter further police harassment, and if he talked back he could be convicted of "resisting arrest." For such incidents, a field contact report is kept by local precincts, which list names, descriptions and associates of people who act "suspiciously," but have not actually broken the law.[107] Since the police are highly suspicious of the poor, especially racial minorities, they tend to be well represented in these reports.

Given the values and practices of lawyers, judges and policemen, it is not difficult to understand why the poor regard the law with hostility and suspicion. More than does medicine and at least as much as education, it contributes to the maintenance and perpetuation of American poverty.

SOCIAL WORKERS AND WELFARE WORKERS

Initially, one might suppose that social work would differ from the other professions in its concern for helping the disadvantaged. However, analysis of its values and practices indicates that it, too, shares the basic American values which maintain and perpetuate poverty. There is a distinct line between social workers who are trained professionals but have little contact with welfare cases, and welfare workers who handle the nation's case load, but have rarely been trained professionally.

SOCIAL WORK TRAINING

Several factors within social work have distracted the profession from a concern for social action to eliminate factors that maintain and perpetuate poverty. One has been the growth of institutional operations. Social workers have been caught in bureaucratic routines that frustrate initiatives for change. Initially led by social reformers such as Jane Addams, the profession soon became dominated by Freudianism.[108] This fit well into the individualistic biases of our society (which perhaps explains why other psychoanalytic theories have not been as popular in America). Freudianism emphasizes "individual readjustment" rather than social reform. Thus, the training of social workers has prepared them to see poverty as an individual problem, ignoring the impact of socioeconomic and political factors, or those of pervasive discriminatory values.

A further deficiency is that the profession has failed to train students for dealing with public assistance.[109] Classroom work has not compensated for the background that students (mostly white and middle class) lack in understanding the poor or racial minorities. Training has avoided problems of legislative animosity and limitations of available public funds, leaving students naively unprepared for the political world in which they will have to function. Not only has the education lacked rigor but with the number of schools easily available, no previous experience has been necessary. Little research has been required, as training has traditionally emphasized interpersonal relations rather than disciplinary competence. As a result, schools of social work have tended to attract less able students and have ill prepared them for understanding and functioning in the area of public assistance.[110]

Moreover, the profession has been more concerned with its own drive for status and recognition than with social action.[111] As do policemen or teachers, social workers use their profession as a means to climb socially from blue-collar or working-class status to white-collar "professional." But less status and recognition has been attained by that profession than by others (teaching, law, or medicine), partly due to its association with "undesirables" like the poor and racial minorities. Social workers are thus inhibited from championing the causes of these undesirables by their own needs for status and recognition.

These deficiencies and the higher salaries available elsewhere cause most trained social workers to go into private institutions or into industrial and business programs rather than to seek employment with public welfare agencies. Thus, the vast majority of welfare workers have received no specific education for their work.

WELFARE WORKERS

Ill-trained welfare workers tend to be ineffectual, insensitive or hostile, as expressed in a number of specific forms:

1) *Guardians of the Public Purse*—the following interview for example with the Welfare Commissioner of a large mid-western city indicates some motivations and hostilities toward the poor:

Q. But you have few people who initially are motivated into a helping profession? A. Damn few . . . many enter the department 'as guardians of the public purse.' They are adversaries of the people on relief. I'm sure you must have found in your Buffalo experience that some of these boys with you said, 'That son-of-a-bitch isn't going to get any more from me.' Now that's a very crucial problem in public welfare. That's very, very tough. He reads in the newspaper that this is a dirty damn business we're in here . . . with chiselers and illegitimate children. It's just more respectable to agree with them.

Q. What do you do to change this attitude? A. Well, not enough.[112]

2) *Unwillingness to fit program to need*—programs and methods have been so shaped by the middle-class values of welfare workers that they have been placed in an unnecessary strait jacket. Far more could have been done with the limited available resources, but services have often been ineffectual because of the manner in which they have been presented to the poor. As one writer noted—

. . . it is not uncommon, therefore, to find ourselves in the embarrassing situation best described by the policeman who finds a dead horse on Kosciusko Street. He has a report to write, but can't spell Kosciusko. His solution is to drag the horse over to First Street so that he can write the report. We have been dragging the problems of the poor over to our middle-class methodology without adequate results. Often we find that when we move in with some of our services the people do not flock to them. There results a gap between the availability and the usability of resources.[113]

3) *The Adversary Relationship*—the Report of the National Advisory Commission on Civil Disorders aptly sums up the hostilities between social workers and their clients—

A source of tension is the brittle relationship that exists between many welfare workers and the poor. The cumulative abrasive effects of the low levels of assistance, the complicated eligibility requirements, the continuing efforts that constitute flagrant invasions of privacy have often brought about an adversary relationship between the caseworker and the recipient family. This is intensified by the fact that the investigative requirements not only force continuing confrontations but, in those states where the same worker performs both investigative and service functions, leave the worker little time to provide service.[114]

These various expressions of hostility, insensitivity and ineffectuality toward the poor stem from preconceptions, inadequate training, an extraordinary workload and from the low priority placed on eliminating degradation and dependency in welfare. Case load is such that the level of service is below that which is needed. Moreover, the recipient-caseworker relationship is unstable because of the high percentage of caseworker resignations and frequent case reassignments. For example, one study of case records suggests that these biographies of dependency were written like an anthology. "Literally dozens of persons contributed a page, two or three. One recipient, on relief for fourteen years, faced seventeen different caseworkers."[115] (Hardly a situation likely to develop a personal base of confidence from which to attack poverty problems.)

High on the list of welfare inadequacies is the fact that while it may succeed in sustaining life, it achieves almost nothing in ameliorating hardship or poverty. Moreover, it is inadequate in a broader sense: relatively few of the nation's poor are receiving even this minor help. Only about one half of the eligible are on welfare rolls, partly due to reluctance to accept the dole, but usually because of the nature of welfare administration which is bureaucratic, impersonal, frustrating and degrading.

The elderly have particular problems as there are relatively few social service personnel trained to deal with them and some social workers feel that not only are such cases more difficult but they lack the long-range benefits which can be derived from working with younger people. As one writer has pointed out, it is consistent with the value system of our society in that service to a group which often cannot reciprocate with concrete achievements is viewed as undesirable, or at least less desirable than service to other groups that can "repay" the social worker's time and effort.[116]

In short, social and welfare workers join the legal, educational and medical professions in helping to maintain and perpetuate American poverty. Even for those professionals who wish to assume responsibility the welfare, legal, educational and medical organizations are so designed that it gives them cause to perpetuate poverty. Thus, these individuals who do not share the widespread racial and class prejudices have had their initiatives stifled.

RESULTING SELF-IMAGE OF THE POOR

Through their contacts with the professions, particularly education, and through their experiences with public policy and the mass media, the poor have been socialized into an image of poverty that shapes their own self-image. They partake of the values of the mainstream as they, too, are Americans.

In addition, there are the corrosive effects of poverty on personality development, which have been fully documented in a variety of sources.[117] These studies agree that the consequence of prolonged poverty is a pervasive hopelessness and depression resulting from the severe frustrations and rejections experienced by the poor in American society. Apathy and alienation are the inevitable psychological adaptations made by the poor to the high stress, frustrating, dangerous world in which they experience daily helplessness, deprivation, insecurity and limited alternatives. Such personality disruption is vastly magnified when the problems of racial discrimination are added. Studies of black poor reflect the degree to which this affects their capacity to function in the broader society.[118]

Given the fact of the objective deterioration and physical ugliness that characterize so much of the ghetto, the chances for the dominance of the psychological negatives in its products are increased. In fact, the pathological characteristics of the ghetto community determine its atmosphere and tend to perpetuate themselves through cumulative deterioration and isolation.

This self-perpetuating community pathology provides the reality basis which reinforces the negative self-image of individuals and confirms their feeling and the fact of their impotence.[119]

One consequence of this negative self-image, alienation and apathy is that the poor are incapacitated from developing their own alternatives to prevailing public values and policy. In the absence of alternatives presented by the poor, the values of the mainstream reign supreme.

Notes

1. ROBERT H. EBERT, M.D., "Foreword" in JOHN KOSA, AARON ANTONOVSKY and IRVING ZOLA, eds., *Poverty and Health: A Sociological Analysis* (Cambridge, Mass.: Harvard University Press, 1969), pp. vi–vii.
2. *Hunger, U.S.A.*; DR. ARNOLD SCHAEFER, Director of a National Nutrition Survey, testimony before the United States Senate Committee on Nutrition and Human Needs, reported in *The New York Times* April 28, 1970, 20:4.
3. *A Report on Health and Medical Care in Poverty Areas of Chicago and Proposals for Improvement*, Chicago Board of Health, Planning Staff of the Health Planning Project, Board of Health, Chicago (1965), pp. 24–25.
4. MONROE LERNER, "Social Differences in Physical Health," in KOSA, ANTONOVSKY and ZOLA, eds., *Poverty and Health: A Sociological Analysis*, pp. 98–99.
5. HURLEY, *Poverty & Mental Retardation: A Causal Relationship*, p. 132.
6. *Ibid.*, p. 132.
7. U.S. National Center for Health Statistics, "Disability Days, United States, July 1963–June 1964," *Vital Statistics: Data From the National Health Survey*, ser. 10, no. 24 (Washington, D.C.: U. S. Government Printing Office, 1965), pp. 8, 29–33.
8. LERNER, "Social Differences in Physical Health," pp. 68–112.
9. WESLEY D. YOUNG, "Dental Health," in Commission on the Survey of Dentistry in the United States, *Survey of Dentistry Final Report*, American Council on Education, Washington, D. C. (1961).
10. LOLA M. IRELAN, "Health Practices of the Poor," in LOLA M. IRELAN, ed., *Low Income Life Styles* (Washington, D. C.: U. S. Government Printing Office, 1966), p. 54; MARC FRIED, "Social Differences in Mental Health," in KOSA, ANTONOVSKY and ZOLA, eds., *Poverty and Health: A Sociological Analysis*, pp. 113–167.
11. GEORGE JAMES, "Poverty as an Obstacle to Health Progress in Our Cities," *American Journal of Public Health*, 55 (November 1965), 1763.
12. JACK T. CONWAY, "The Beneficiary, the Consumer—What He Needs and Wants," *American Journal of Public Health*, 55 (November 1963).

99

13. Louis L. Knowles and Kenneth Prewitt, *Institutional Racism in America* (Englewood Cliffs, N. J.: Prentice-Hall, 1969), Table III, p. 98.
14. Study of Watts by the University of Southern California, cited in *Ibid.*, p. 99.
15. G. James, "Poverty as an Obstacle to Health Progress in Our Cities," p. 1759.
16. Irelan, "Health Practices of the Poor," pp. 7–9.
17. Milton Roemer and Arnold Kisch, "Health, Poverty and the Medical Mainstream," in Warner Bloomberg and Henry Schmandt, eds., *Power, Poverty and Urban Policy*, p. 200.
18. *The New York Times*, June 21, 1967, 20:3.
19. Oliver Garceau, *The Political Life of the American Medical Association* (Cambridge, Mass.: Harvard University Press, 1941); Stanley Kelley, *Professional Public Relations and Political Power* (Baltimore, Md.: Johns Hopkins Press, 1956), chap. 3; Eli Ginsberg and Miriam Ostow, *Men, Money and Medicine* (New York: Columbia University Press, 1970); Eliot Friedson, *Professional Dominance: The Social Structure of Medical Care* (New York: Atherton Press, 1970).
20. Ginsberg and Ostow, *Men, Money and Medicine.*
21. *Hunger, U.S.A.*
22. For a review of the literature on this see Knowles & Prewitt, *Institutional Racism in America*, chap. 7. See also William Grier & Price Cobbs, *Black Rage* (New York: Basic Books, 1968).
23. Irelan, "Health Practices of the Poor"; and Hurley, *Poverty & Mental Retardation: A Causal Relationship.*
24. Hurley, *Poverty & Mental Retardation: A Causal Relationship.*
25. *Ibid.*, p. 175.
26. Esther Spencer, "Medicaid Lessons and Warnings," *Social Policy*, vol. 1 (January/February, 1971), pp. 47–51.
27. S.M. Miller and Frank Riessman, *Social Class and Social Policy* (New York: Basic Books, 1968), p. 80.
28. Patricia Cayo Sexton, *Education and Income* (New York: Viking Press, 1966), pp. 205–206.
29. Study by Joel B. Montague reported in *Ibid.*, p. 207.
30. For example, see the 1969 masterplan of the Board of Education of the City of New York, which shows a majority of the city's public school students to be black and Puerto Rican, but most of these students who graduate receive commercial, vocational or general diplomas, whereas whites receive the vast majority of academic diplomas (necessary for college attendance).
31. Leonore Epstein, "Migratory Farm Workers" in Will and Vatter, p. 112.
32. Hurley, *Poverty & Mental Retardation: A Causal Relationship*, chap. 9.
33. Moore, *The Slaves We Rent*, chap. 4.
34. Epstein, "Migratory Farm Workers," p. 113.
35. Caudill, *Night Comes to the Cumberlands*, pp. 336–347.
36. Reported in *The New York Times* (March 3, 1970), 24:1.
37. Sexton, *Education and Income.*
38. *Ibid.*, pp. 124, 216–222; James S. Coleman, *et. al.*, *Equality of Educational Opportunity* (Washington, D. C.: U. S. Government Printing Office, 1966).
39. Sexton, *Spanish Harlem*, chap. 5.
40. Sexton, *Education and Income*, p. 118.

41. *Ibid.*, p. 134; and HURLEY, *Poverty & Mental Retardation: A Causal Relationship*, chap. 7.

42. Report by the NAACP Legal Defense and Educational Fund, Inc. and the Washington Research Project of the Southern Center for Studies in Public Policy, reported in *The New York Times*, November 9, (1969), 1:1.

43. CAUDILL, *Night Comes to the Cumberlands*, pp. 336–337.

44. For example, see NAT HENTOFF, *Our Children Are Dying* (New York: Viking Press, 1967); JONATHAN KOZOL, *Death at an Early Age* (New York: Houghton Mifflin, 1968).

45. SEXTON, *Education and Income*, p. 60.

46. ELIZABETH M. EDDY, *Walk The White Line* (Garden City, N.Y.: Doubleday, 1967).

47. HURLEY, *Poverty & Mental Retardation: A Causal Relationship*.

48. EDGAR LITT, "Civic Education, Community Norms, and Political Indoctrination," *American Sociological Review*, 28 (February, 1963), 69–75.

49. KOZOL, *Death at an Early Age*, p. 31.

50. Examples of the literature include the following previously cited works: HENTOFF, KOZOL, EDDY, KNOWLES & PREWITT, HURLEY, and GRIER & COBBS. See Also KENNETH B. CLARK, *Prejudice and Your Child* (Boston: Beacon Press, 1967); KENNETH B. CLARK, *Dark Ghetto* (New York: Harper & Row, 1967); CHARLES GLOCK and ELLEN SIEGELMAN, eds., *Prejudice, U.S.A.* (New York: Frederick Praeger, 1969).

51. S. STEINER, *Indians*; VINE DELORIA, *Custer Died For Your Sins* (New York: Macmillan, 1969); DAVID HENNINGER and NANCY ESPOSITO, "Indian Schools: Regimented Non-Education," *The New Republic* 160 (February 15, 1969), pp. 18–21.

52. SAMORA, *La Raza*; S. STEINER, *Mexicans*; JOHN BURMA, ed., *Mexican-Americans in the United States* (New York: Harper & Row, 1970); *The New York Times*, September 4, 1970, 20:1.

53. THOMAS, *Down These Mean Streets*; BURMA, *Mexican Americans in the U.S.*; SEXTON, *Spanish Harlem*; and SUTTLES, *The Social Order of the Slum*.

54. GRIER and COBBS, *Black Rage*, p. 132.

55. *Youth in the Ghetto*, reported in Harlem Youth Opportunities Unlimited, Inc. (New York: Orans Press, 1964), p. 237. [Hereafter cited as H.A.R.Y.O.U.]

56. CLARK, *Dark Ghetto*; HURLEY, *Poverty & Mental Retardation: A Causal Relationship*; ALBERT H. YEE, study reported in *Transaction*, 7 (July/August, 1970), 10–13.

57. *Ibid.*

58. ZONA FAIRBANKS HOSTETLER, "Poverty and the Law" in Seligman, ed., *Poverty as a Public Issue*.

59. The major research in this area is CAPLOVITZ, *The Poor Pay More*.

60. *Ibid.*; MILTON J. HUBER, "The Poor in the Market Place," in Bloomberg & Schmandt, eds., *Power, Poverty and Urban Policy*.

61. *Ibid.*

62. ALVIN L. SCHOOR, "Housing the Poor" in BLOOMBERG & SCHMANDT, eds., *Power, Poverty, and Urban Policy*.

63. GEORGE STERNLIEB, *The Tenement Landlord* (New Brunswick, N. J.: Rutgers University Press, 1966).

64. CAPLOVITZ, *The Poor Pay More*, p. 171.

65. PHILIP A. STOHR, "The German System of Legal Aid: An Alternative Approach," in tenBROEK, ed., *The Law of the Poor*.

66. ALBERT A. EHRENZWEIG, "Reimbursement of Counsel Fees and the Great Society," in tenBROEK.

67. HOSTETLER, *"Poverty and the Law"*, pp. 185–187.

68. J. SKELLY WRIGHT, "The Courts Have Failed the Poor," *The New York Times Magazine* (March 9, 1969), 102.

69. Alameda County, California Bar Association schedule of suggested minimum fees for a criminal case tried before a U.S. District Court.

70. *Poverty and the Administration of Federal Criminal Justice*, Report of the Attorney General's Committee on Poverty and the Administration of Criminal Justice, U.S. Department of Justice (1963).

71. LEE SILVERSTEIN, *Defense of the Poor*, National Report of the American Bar Foundation (1965), p. 25.

72. *Ibid.*, pp. 54–55.

73. Telephone conversation recorded by Ernesto Collazo with lawyer from the Bronx criminal branch of the Legal Aid Society, from an unpublished college term paper on law and poverty by Mr. Collazo.

74. HERMA HILL KAY & IRVING PHILIPS, "Poverty and the Law of Child Custody," and HASSELTINE B. TAYLOR, "Guardianship or 'Permanent Placement of Children' ", in tenBROEK, ed., *The Law of the Poor*.

75. MONRAD G. PAULSEN, "Juvenile Courts, Family Courts, and the Poor Man," in tenBROEK, ed., *The Law of the Poor*; DAVID L. BAZELON, "Justice for Juveniles," *The New Republic* (April 22, 1967), 13–16.

76. *Poverty and the Administration of Federal Criminal Justice*, p. 58.

77. RONALD GOLDFARB, *Ransom: A Critique of the American Bail System* (New York: Harper & Row, 1965), p. 42.

78. MONRAD PAULSEN, "Pre-Trial Release in the United States," *Columbia Law Review*, 66 (January–April, 1966), 113.

79. *Poverty and the Administration of Federal Criminal Justice*, pp. 101–3.

80. *The New York Times*, August 14, 1970, 1:8.

81. *Ibid.*, 14:2–3.

82. *Race Makes the Difference*, Southern Regional Council, Atlanta (1969).

83. "Federal Enforcement of School Desegregation," A Report of the United States Commission on Civil Rights (September 11, 1969).

84. MOORE, *The Slaves We Rent; The New York Times*, August 17, 1970, 1:1.

85. KENNETH DOLBEARE, *Trial Courts in Urban Politics* (New York: John Wiley & Sons, 1967).

86. The Boise, Idaho *Intermountain Observer*, August 2, 1969, 6:1.

87. *The New York Times*, March 23, 1970, 43:1.

88. *Ibid.*

89. *The New York Times*, July 7, 1968, 34:4.

90. *The New York Times*, July 5, 1968, 1:3.

91. *Report of the National Advisory Commission on Civil Disorders* (New York: Bantam Books, 1968), p. 17.

92. NICHOLAS ALEX, *Black in Blue* (New York: Appleton-Century-Crofts, 1969), p. 9.

93. *Ibid.*, p. 10.

94. ARTHUR NIEDERHOFFER, *Behind the Shield* (New York: Doubleday, 1967), p. 130.

95. *Ibid.*, p. 107.

96. PAUL G. CHEVIGNY, *Police Power* (New York: Pantheon Press, 1969).

97. DONALD BLACK & ALBERT REISS, *Studies of Crime and Law Enforcement in Major Metropolitan Areas* (Washington, D.C.: U.S. Government Printing Office, 1965), p. 32.

98. BYRON LINDSLEY, "The Quality of Law Enforcement," *Civil Rights Digest*, 2 (Spring 1969), 41.

99. Testimony of Paul G. Chevigny, reported in New York Civil Liberties Union, *Civil Liberties in New York*, 17 (December 1968–Jan. 1969), 2–4.

100. JAMES WILSON, *Varieties of Police Behavior* (Cambridge, Mass.: Harvard University Press, 1968), p. 141.

101. *Ibid.*, p. 140.

102. ROBERT FOGELSON, "From Resentment to Confrontation," *Political Science Quarterly* 43 (June 1968), 221.

103. WILSON, *Varieties of Police Behavior*, p. 172.

104. *Ibid.*, p. 190.

105. *Ibid.*, p. 200.

106. *Ibid.*

107. *Ibid.*, p. 12.

108. CHAMBERS, *Seedtime of Reform.*

109. G. STEINER, *Social Insecurity.*

110. *Ibid.*

111. *Ibid.*

112. EDGAR MAY, *The Wasted Americans* (New York: Harper & Row; 1964), p. 106.

113. NATHAN COHEN, "A National Program for the Improvement of Welfare Services and the Reduction of Welfare Dependency" in MARGARET GORDON, ed., *Poverty in America* (San Francisco: Chandler, 1965) pp. 293–294.

114. *Report of the National Advisory Commission on Civil Disorders*, p. 460.

115. MAY, *The Wasted Americans*, p. 109.

116. IRVING ROSTOW, *Social Integration of the Aged* (New York: Free Press, 1967), p. 48.

117. One recent major work on the subject is HURLEY, *Poverty & Mental Retardation: A Causal Relationship.* A brief summary of recent research on subcultures of poverty may be found in CATHERINE S. CHILMAN, *Growing Up Poor*, U.S. Department of Health, Education and Welfare, Washington, D.C. (1966). Also see MILTON GREENBLATT, ed., *Poverty and Mental Health*, Psychiatric Research Report no. 21, The American Psychiatric Association (January 1967).

118. GRIER & COBBS, *Black Rage*; Clark, *Dark Ghetto*; STOKELY CARMICHAEL & CHARLES V. HAMILTON, *Black Power* (New York: Vintage, 1967); and ANDREW BILLINGSLEY, *Black Families in White America* (Englewood Cliffs, N.J.: Prentice-Hall, 1968), p. 146.

119. H.A.R.Y.O.U., pp. 11–12.

FIVE

Economic and Political Factors that Maintain and Perpetuate American Poverty

Existing economic inequities have been reinforced and increased by accelerating changes in American economic organization. The political system has also reinforced and increased existing inequities as a result of the class bias of voting and political participation, the decentralization of its decision-making centers, and the increasing professionalization of the bureaucracy. The nation's economic and political organization, then, has done its share in partially maintaining and perpetuating American poverty.

ACCELERATING CHANGE IN AMERICAN ECONOMIC ORGANIZATION

At present the two dominant economic processes are the breakdown of competitive capitalism for most sectors of the economy, and a shift from a manufacturing to a service economy which requires higher levels of skill and education. The effect of both processes, supplemented by law and social custom, has reinforced and increased inequities, leading to an accelerating growth in the number of persons on welfare.

SOCIALISM FOR THE RICH BUT FREE ENTERPRISE FOR THE POOR

The flexibility necessary for a system based on a market economy no longer exists here because major elements of the economic system such as corporations, organized labor, large-scale farming and the professions have avoided market restraints. Corporations have been able to escape these restraints because of: the manner in which government policies have assisted business; development of oligopolies and conglomerates; and their relations with organized labor.

The impact of government policies on the poor will be pursued, not their value to other groups in the country. If the reader considers that value to be high, but recognizes the policy's adverse effect upon poor people, he should consider whether it might not be possible to formulate policy to compensate the poor for that adverse effect. (Naturally, if he considers the policy to hold "no redeeming social value" then he should consider ending it.)

Government policies assist business through numerous subsidies. For example, the government pays oil and mineral depletion allowances, meaning that as a matter of public policy the United States rewards businessmen for exhausting its natural resources. Thus, the owner sells a natural resource for profit and receives a tax rebate from the government because he no longer has what he sold. Another form of subsidy is the heavy expenditure on aid to transportation, which thereby indirectly subsidizes industries that depend upon it: the merchant marine, highway construction, airport facilities, canals and railroads. A further form of government subsidy is the large number of defense contracts and funds for research and development upon which much of American industry depends. To the degree that tax laws benefit the well-to-do they provide a form of government subsidy, too. The preferred tax status of capital gains, deferred-compensation plans for corporate executives, the stock option as a means to avoid taxation, gifts and trusts to avoid inheritance taxes, and expense-account living have resulted in two basic trends:

. . . the growing tax burden of the low- and middle-income classes, and the huge disparity between theoretical and actual tax rates for the wealthy. The conclusion is inescapable: Taxation has not mitigated the fundamentally unequal distribution of income. If anything it has perpetuated inequality by heavily taxing the low- and middle-income groups—those least able to bear its burden.[1]

The history of a great deal of government regulation of business reveals that it was enacted at the *request* of businessmen in order to restrict competition. For example, businesses want licensing requirements to prevent competition by restricting the number of licenses issued. Typically, those groups that are most powerful in a particular area establish the requirements for that area, which the government enforces. Similarly, public utility regulations permit the established power, telephone or transportation companies to operate without facing competition, and fair trade laws reduce price competition by restricting discounts on products.

The oligopoly is a basic fact of American corporate life in which very few large firms account for the bulk of production in most major industries. Over half the needed products in their respective fields, for example, are produced by General Motors in the automotive field, U.S. Steel in steel, Alcoa in aluminum, and Goodyear in rubber. There is an oligopolistic pattern in fields as diverse as television receivers, cigarettes, plate glass, antibiotics, aircraft, cellulose plastics or meat packing, and the trend is growing.[2] Even if their competitors tried to undersell them, these leaders would have the resources to carry on a price war to destroy their competition. Their competitors, thus, find it economically expedient to follow the leaders, resulting in "administered pricing"—prices determined by management policy rather than in response to supply and demand. If a firm can manage its prices, it can manage its profits as well, thereby exempting it from the competition of the market system.

Another effective means to avoid the consequences of a market system is to develop a conglomerate, which diversifies corporations by acquiring other totally *unrelated* corporations. This form has had a tremendous, accelerating growth. The corporation as a whole, then, is not dependent on fluctuation of demand for a given product. Price competition becomes irrelevant because a conglomerate can invest such large sums of money for the distribution and advertisement of a product that almost regardless of quality it can obtain a share of the market from those who only manufacture for that one market. A theoretical case in point: if General Motors were to diversify by purchasing a relatively mediocre ice cream company, it would be able to spend enough on advertising and distribution to gain a share of the ice cream market from specialists who make a higher quality product.

The major segments of organized labor (strong unions in core industries and craft unions in the building trades) are able to cause employers to come to terms with them, merely passing increased costs on to the consumer. Thereby, organized labor avoids the restraints of the market system. Unions in core industries such as transportation, steel or automobiles can bring employers to terms either through unity in dealing with scattered, small employers (truckers or dock workers) or through power in numbers and wealth (steel or automotive workers). Craft unions are able to regulate admission to their craft through control of apprenticeship programs. Through regional organization dealing with small, numerous employers they are also able to regulate work rules, hours and wages.

The farm parity system is a subsidy from which large-scale farmers are best able to profit: They put land out of use to qualify for acreage controls. Therefore, larger farms naturally receive more parity payment (particularly since the specific allocations under government formulas are devised by local committees of farmers on which the wealthy farmers are over represented).[3] The relative price stability resulting from the farm parity system enables large-scale farmers to accumulate enough capital to purchase machinery which enables them to produce more from the same land. Although government policy was designed to protect small farmers from major price fluctuations, they have not been the principal beneficiaries as can be seen by their continued migration from rural to urban areas.

The degree to which farm subsidies have benefited the rich may be seen in the following statistics:

While millions of Americans continue to suffer from hunger and thousands of small farmers are forced out of agriculture, large corporations continue to receive a lion's share of federal farm subsidies. Of the 1,210 farms that received payments of $50,000 or more in 1968, about one-fourth were corporate farming operations. More than 80 percent of the subsidies went to fewer than 20 percent of the farms.

Five corporate farming operations received more than $1 million each in 1969. Of these, three were located in Kings County, one of the poorest counties in California in terms of average annual income. J. G. Boswell Company alone received payments totaling $4,370,657. At the same time, one million small farmers averaged less than $400 per year in subsidy payments.[4]

Professionals can avoid the restraints of a market system by restricting entry to their fields and protecting their sources of revenue. Entry is protected for a number of professions (elementary and secondary school teachers, nurses, undertakers, doctors, lawyers or dentists) by their control of licensing regulations. The American Medical Association carefully restricts the number of accredited medical schools.[5] Lawyers are particularly effective in protecting their revenue sources because they are the largest occupational group in all legislatures. They have successfully fought many reforms which would limit them, such as those in no-fault automobile insurance, or reform of probate procedures.

The consequence of these various restrictions is a highly structured, rigid price system, and a noncompetitive market for major sectors of the American economy. Since neither prices nor wages can be cut, continued inflation seems likely without *sustained*, rigid government controls. Thus, the restraint in the market system that deflation or price competition is supposed to provide is nonexistent for large sectors of the economy. Ours is an increasingly inflexible economic system.

There are, however, a few groups (unemployed, elderly on fixed pensions, and non-unionized labor) which lack these hedges, and consequently are affected by the restraints of the market system. For example, although clerical and sales workers are a growing percentage of the work force, there has been a serious downward trend in their relative income level.[6] These factors explain the growing pressures during the 1960s to unionize among groups such as teachers, civil servants and migrant farm workers.

When the various private "welfare" systems available to corporate and union members and professionals, including pensions, health care, sick leave and various "fringe benefits" are totaled, it would appear that the American economic system approximates one of socialism for the rich but free enterprise for the poor. Moreover, government policy provides increasing subsidies as one rises on the economic scale. This was summarized in the following story by Senator Stephen Young of Ohio who suggested that few members of the middle class were aware of just how widespread was government assistance, or how much they took it for granted:

A young man lived . . . in Hamilton County. He attended public school, rode the free school bus, enjoyed the free lunch program.

Following graduation from high school, he entered the Army and upon discharge kept his National Service Life Insurance. He then enrolled in an Ohio university, receiving regularly his GI check. Upon graduation, he married a Public Health nurse, bought a farm in southern Ohio with an FHA loan.

Later going into the feed and hardware business in addition to farming, he secured help from the Small Business Administration when his business faltered. His first baby was born in the county hospital. This was built in part with Hill-Burton federal funds.

Then, he put part of his land under the Eisenhower Soil Bank Program and used the payments for not growing crops to help pay his debts. His parents, elderly by now, were living comfortably in the smaller of his two farm houses, using their Social Security and Old Age Assistance checks. Medicare covered most of their doctor and hospital bills. Lacking electricity at first, he got the Rural Electrification Administration to supply the lines. A loan from the Farmers Home Administration helped clear the land and secure the best from it. That agency suggested building a pond, and the government stocked it with fish.

The government guaranteed him a sale for his farm products. The county public library delivered books to his farm door. He, of course, banked his money in an institution which a federal agency had insured up to $15,000 for every depositor. As the community grew, he signed a petition seeking federal assistance in developing an industrial project to help the economy of his area. About that time, he purchased a business and real estate at the county seat, aided by an FHA loan. His children in college received financial assistance from the Federal Government, his son under the National Defense Student Loan Program and his daughter under the Nurse Training Act. Both lived in dormitories and studied in classrooms paid for with Federal funds. He was elected to office in the local Chamber of Commerce. A little later it was rumored he joined a cell of the John Birch Society and also the Liberty Lobby, both right-wing extremist groups.

He wrote his Senators and congressmen denouncing excessive government spending, Medicare, big government, the United Nations, high taxes, *etc.*, and enclosed John Birch propaganda pamphlets, some containing outlandishly false statements. He wrote:

"I believe in rugged individualism. People should stand on their own feet, not expect government aid. I stand on my own two feet. I oppose all those socialistic trends you have been voting for and demand return to the free enterprise system of our forefathers.

"I and my neighbors intend to vote against you this year."[7]

THE "POST-INDUSTRIAL" REVOLUTION

Economic activity may be classified in three stages. In the primary stage, most people are employed in the extractive functions of farming, fishing, mining, lumbering. In the secondary stage, most people are employed in manufacture which entails processing materials. In the tertiary stage it becomes a service economy in which most people are employed in service industries such as health, education, publishing, advertising, computer services, insurance or finance. The United States underwent its industrial revolution during the late nineteenth and early twentieth centuries, shifting from an economy in which most persons were employed in extractive functions to one in which the majority were employed in manufacture. The "post-industrial" revolution has resulted in equally major social change, whereby the economy shifted from a manufacturing to a service one by the mid-twentieth century. (For example, one of the largest single categories of employment in America today is that of school teacher.)

As a result of the industrial revolution, population began to shift from rural to urban areas. Increasing mechanization of American agriculture was both a response to this drain of rural population and a cause of continued migration. By the end of World War II the majority of Americans lived in metropolitan areas. Major areas of employment in agriculture or mining which had not been substantially affected by automation were the harvesting of cotton, fruits and vegetables, and the mining of coal.

Since the 1950s the shift to a service economy has been growing at an accelerating rate, as has automation in extractive industries and in manufacture. Automation finally reached cotton in the form of the mechanical cotton picker, and coal in the mechanical "joy" drill for mining.[8] These two inventions have produced a labor surplus which cannot find other employment because the skill level is either limited (cotton picking) or highly skilled (coal mining) but not transferable to other fields. Similar mechanization has effected other agricultural areas, and lumbering and fishing. In the present decade automation seems likely to reach the harvesting of fruit and vegetables, replacing migrant laborers with machines.

Secondarily, the shift of unskilled rural population to urban centers was accelerated by government agricultural policy. The farm subsidy program helped to increase urban slums by driving from the land persons without skills which were transferable to urban living. When large-scale farmers retired their least productive land to obtain parity payments they had to limit acreage devoted to production, thereby depriving tenant farmers of employment and acreage to plant grain for themselves and livestock. Moreover, when the prices became stable and wealthy farmers were then able to accumulate enough capital to farm intensively by using machinery, they laid off their workers. Some agricultural change and displacement would naturally have occurred because of mechanization, but the subsidy program speeded up the process, affecting small and tenant farmers, farm laborers and migrants. The resulting impact was felt mostly by Southern blacks.

Within a few decades there was a dramatic shift of blacks who had lived in rural areas of the South, prior to these changes to urban ones. Only about five percent have remained on the farms.[9] Their social dislocation reflected in and reinforced by this mass exodus helped to incite the violent, explosive urban problems that began in 1964 with the Harlem riot and were followed for several years by numerous other such riots around the country.

When this unskilled labor reached the cities it found little opportunity in manufacturing because that sector of the economy had also been shrinking in terms of the percentage of Americans it employed, primarily due to automation. According to the Bureau of Labor Statistics, the number of unskilled jobs is declining so rapidly that by 1975 nearly two-thirds of the national work force will be employed in white collar and service jobs.[10]

Even in those relatively few jobs remaining for unskilled labor, the general economic decentralization that is occurring deeply affects the poor. Many businesses are moving out of central cities into the suburbs for better transportation and more space. As it has become more economical to ship by truck than by rail, manufacturers have had to leave central cities to avoid traffic congestion. In addition, modern manufacturing demands greater space to construct continuous assembly lines, for which land in central cities is too costly when it is available. The significance of these trends for the poor is denial of the few existing job opportunities at their skill level. Nor can they live in the suburbs because of higher costs and widespread discrimination against racial minorities.

In the past two decades a shift of population within metropolitan areas has occurred: The working class moved to the inner suburbs and the middle class, to the further suburbs, leaving in the central cities the disadvantaged who are increasingly black, Mexican-American and Puerto

Rican. So these minorities were surrounded by suburbs inhabited by the whites. Although the 1970 census indicated nonwhite suburban growth, substantial racial barriers still exist in much of suburbia.

Since the 1950s, Americans have depended heavily upon private transportation, have limited mass transit, but are expending large sums for highway construction instead. Except for New York City, and to a lesser degree Boston and Washington, D.C., most Eastern cities have only struggling, frequently defunct, bus lines of limited service. Beyond the East coast there is little effective mass transit. This adds to the disadvantages of the black, Puerto Rican and Mexican-American by not providing adequate transportation between suburban jobs and their housing.[11]

Since recent economic trends have resulted in changes in the level of skill necessary for work, more education is required. Increasingly, there is very little work available for which simple brawn and willingness to work is adequate. Presently, it is hard to make even an *adequate* living without either a high school education or an aptitude for a specialized skill in an expanding industry, which requires formal training. There is a growing need for clerical workers, professionals and paraprofessionals. The situation was summarized by one expert in testimony before a Senate committee:

During at least the past two decades, the growth patterns of our affluent society have created vastly different conditions in the upper and lower sectors of our labor market. Less-skilled and less-educated workers have faced conditions of shrinking job opportunities and chronic looseness in their part of the labor market . . . hundreds of thousands of them, perceiving the search for work as futile, have stopped looking . . . higher-skilled and better-educated workers have lived in a quite different world—one with abundant and growing opportunity, with falling unemployment rates, with a chronically tight labor market.[12]

These accelerating changes in American economic organization have accompanied and contributed to severe strain in American social organization.

The significance of these demographic trends for social organization may be seen in the fact that traditional organization has been severely undermined in rural areas and small towns, and has not developed fully in many suburbs because of their rapid growth. A breakdown of social organization leads to increasing social problems such as drug addiction, juvenile delinquency, crime and civil disorders. The shifts within metropolitan areas have led to greater racial segregation and to severe economic crises for the central cities. At the same time that increasing percentages of dependent persons have been draining central city resources, the loss of industry and population to the suburbs has handicapped their financial base. Thus, central cities have been unable to cope with the need for services, such as education. This, in turn, has further contributed to the middle-class exodus to the suburbs, resulting in a vicious cycle for the poor. As the middle class leaves because public services have deteriorated, those very services deteriorate more, thereby further handicapping the poor who are dependent upon them.

DECENTRALIZATION OF THE AMERICAN POLITICAL SYSTEM

Just as the economic and social systems have tended to maintain and perpetuate poverty, so has the American political system. Three aspects of the political system are relevant in this regard: the class bias of voting and political participation, the multiplicity of decision-making centers, and the impact of an increasingly professionalized bureaucracy.

CLASS BIAS OF VOTING AND POLITICAL PARTICIPATION

Inevitably, business and professional groups are more effectively organized to protect their economic interests than are other groups in American society; it is inherent in the logic of collective action that they will have a substantial influence on the formulation of public policy. This was made clear by Mancur Olson in the following terms.[13]

People will *not* automatically organize and work for their common interest because a collective good is such that *all* members of a group will benefit from it, whether they have worked for it or not. (For example, all blacks benefit from the desegregation decision of the Supreme Court without paying dues to the National Association for the Advancement of Colored People which brought the case to judgment.) Consequently, rational, self-interested individuals will *not* act together to achieve their common group interest. Therefore, groups can only be mobilized if they have the authority and capacity to coerce their members to support them, or if they have a source of positive inducements to cause their members to mobilize. Thus, Olson found that large, powerful economic lobbies were actually *by-products* of organizations that obtained their strength and support because they performed some function *in addition* to lobbying for collective goods.

Business and industries are more organized and obtain more individual, specific benefits for their members than other groups. The degree of organization and success in obtaining group ends inevitably diminishes as it moves down the socio-economic scale. The implications of elite influence on government policy are thus inherent in the logic of collective action, because the poor constitute a large, unorganized group. As Professor Olson suggested:

Since relatively small groups will frequently be able voluntarily to act in support of their common interests, and since large groups normally will not be able to do so, the outcome of the political struggle among the various groups in society will not be symmetrical.[14]

Participation in organized groups correlates directly with socio-economic status because of the type of resources (money, leisure) and skills (verbal, organizational, and informational) necessary for organizational activity. As E. E. Schattschneider noted: "The flaw in the pluralist heaven is that the heavenly chorus sings with a strong upper-class accent."[15] This is reflected in the pattern of American voting behavior.

A series of formal obstacles to voting exist that have a disproportionate impact on the poor. Migrant laborers, for instance, are the major category of persons disfranchised by the brief residence requirements currently established by each state. A major legal obstacle is the requirement of formal registration prior to election day with each state establishing its own administrative procedures. Thus, a state wishing to limit registration of the poor may set the date for registration months before the time when a political campaign will arouse voter interest. It may limit registration to hours and places inconvenient for working people and ghetto residents. In addition, it may turn literacy requirements and proof of age and residence into major stumbling blocs, harassing voters and inhibiting registration. Annual personal registration may be required so that the obstacle course must be run prior to each election. All of these practices have been frequently used in the South, as well as in other areas of the country.

The Voting Rights Act of 1964 has limited overt examples of harassment, but administrative measures can still effectively limit registration and voting.[16] Analysis of their impact points out that:

. . . the magnitude of the effects of legal restrictions on voting depends on the degree to which the individual voter is motivated to work. If his motivation is high, formal facilitation or inhibition of his behavior is relatively ineffective: if his motivation is low, his actual performance may be greatly affected by the same legal forms.[17]

Motivation, then, plays the crucial role in determining the degree to which eligible voters will overcome formal obstacles, and motivation is related to factors that correlate highly with socio-economic status. This explains why upper middle-class, white Americans are the predominant voters, whereas voting turnout among the poor is particularly low, and that of blue collar or lower middle-class voters is low relative to their proportion in the adult population.

The key factors in voter motivation have been found to be information, a sense of political effectiveness and a sense of citizen duty.[18] All three depend on education and membership in organized groups.[19] A case in point: American voters gain relevant information about times, dates and places of registration and voting and election issues and candidates primarily from the mass media, organized interest groups and political parties. Repeated studies of American voting behavior have shown that membership in organized groups is particularly important because a group will make one aware of issues in the media and help one to interpret the media and to understand the actions of the different political parties.[20] The group also tries to influence what the media will cover and the manner in which it will be covered, what positions political parties will take and which candidates will be chosen. The poor, then, who have had little or no organization lack the means to influence media and party policy information for both registering and voting.

Since organized interest groups provide the major stimulation to voter registration, registered voters in America definitely do not represent the population as a whole. They are disproportionately whites of business or professional status, and male. They are also much older than the majority of Americans. The advanced age of registered voters may be partially explained by the Constitutional provision that prohibits voting by those under the age of eighteen, and by the fact that persons between eighteen and thirty have a tendency to be politically inactive. This may be explained by the fact that membership in organized interest groups (and its attendant influence toward greater attention to the media and identification with political parties) increases with age from eighteen to the middle years. After sixty-five there is a marked drop in voting due to factors such as illness, personal handicaps, and retirement (with its consequent loss of membership in organized groups). Thus, 59 percent of registered voters in America are between the ages of thirty-five and sixty-four.

This disproportion is even greater in state and local elections. Therefore, in their constituent base, state and local governments are even further divorced from the poor than is the national government. Significantly, most programs dealing with the poor are administered by state or local governments.

Motivation plays a further role in getting those who have overcome all the formal restrictions to actually cast ballots on election day. Even among those who are eligible, a large proportion do not actually vote. For example, 15 million registered voters did not vote in the 1968 Presidential election.[21] A lower percentage of voter turnout is typical for all elective offices. In short, the poor do not vote because of:

disenfranchisement through technical residence and registration requirements; language barriers for those whose native tongue is not English, or rural blacks and whites who speak an American dialect and are hampered in verbal communication;

social and economic pressures;

lack of political information due to their inattention to politics (having only limited access to media or organizations), and due to the failure of American education which has left them unequipped to understand the information they do receive; and

their own well-founded cynicism about what the government will do for them.

The sharp contrast between characteristics of the American poor and the electorate are shown in Table 3, but it does not tell the entire

Table 5.1

COMPARISON OF DOMINANT CHARACTERISTICS OF AMERICAN VOTERS IN NATIONAL ELECTIONS (1968) WITH THOSE OF THE AMERICAN POOR (1967)

	Dominant Characteristics of American Voters in National Elections, 1968	Dominant Characteristics of American Poor, 1967
AGE	median age 45 years[1] 58.8% voters between 35 & 65	41% under 18[2] 18% over 65[3]
NONWHITE	8.5%[4]	32.2%[5]
EDUCATION	median of school attendance is 12 yrs (completion of high school)[6] 20.7% have education beyond high school	8 years or less[7]
FAMILY INCOME	median income $7,500–$9,999 over 30% earned $10,000 or over[8]	100% below poverty line of $3,410 annual family income, $1,600 annual income for unattached individual
OCCUPATIONAL STATUS	primarily business and professional	primarily unskilled labor, domestic, unemployed

1U. S. Bureau of the Census, *Statistical Abstracts of the United States: 1969* (90th edition), Washington, D. C., 1969, Table #536, p. 371.
2*Ibid.*, Table #484, p. 328. In 1967, of a total population of 26.1 million poor persons, 10.7 million were children under 18.
31968 as reported by the Committee for Economic Development, "Improving the Public Welfare System," April 1970, p. 26.
4*Abstracts*, Table #536, p. 371.
5*Ibid.*, Table #484, p. 328.
6*Ibid.*, Table #536.
7Council of Economic Advisers, *Economic Report of the President Together With the Annual Report*, January, 1964.
8*Abstracts*, Table #536.

story of class bias in American voting. In most cases, the vote on election day is less significant than on primary day, because party primaries decide which candidate will run in the election. Since one party dominates in most legislative districts (city, state and national) and many constituencies for mayors and governors, the choice of the dominant party's candidate in a primary is tantamount to his election. Information about time, place, candidates and issues is limited, and voter turnout is low compared to election day. Consequently, organized groups are highly motivated to get their members to the polls on primary day, as a concerted effort by small numbers of organized voters can have an impact on party nomination disproportionate to their strength in the electorate. As a result this voter turnout is even more biased than on election day in favor of white, business and professional, middle-aged males.[22]

In assessing the significance of class bias in voter turnout the basis on which voters cast their ballots must be considered. While subsequent elections may produce more variations in these percentages, the basic import of a massive study of the American electorate by the staff of the University of Michigan Survey Research Center appears to be a fairly representative description of voters' levels of issue conceptualization.[23] It found that only about 15 percent of the electorate voted on the basis of ideology or near-ideology.[24] A large number, approximately 17 percent, voted on the basis of no issue content whatsoever (*e.g.*, party organization, candidate orientation). Almost half, 45 percent, voted on the basis of individual perceptions of group benefits in the election. The final major category, 23 percent cast their ballots on the basis of their assessments of the "goodness" or "badness" of the times. For many this was a less sophisticated version of voting on the basis of group benefits. Interviews found that: "Typically, there is a perception of the economic state of the immediate family, which is an index of the 'goodness' or 'badness' of the times."[25]

Table 5.2

SUMMARY OF LEVELS OF ISSUE CONCEPTUALIZATION OF
AMERICAN VOTERS

Ideology	15%
Group Benefits	45%
Nature of the Times	23%
No Issue Content	17%
(includes party and candidate orientation)	

Thus, those who do vote tend to cast their ballots primarily on the basis of a more or less sophisticated assessment of their own group benefits. Since representatives of this group are those who formulate public policy, it is necessary to consider the degree to which they reflect constituency values to understand public attempts to deal with the poor. There are many legislators and executives who desire to do what they believe is best for their entire constituency, not just its organized members. But a problem arises: because representatives themselves are not poor, and the unorganized poor do not offer them alternatives to those policies provided by large organized political lobbies, they may be completely unaware of the impact that their policies will have on the poor. Moreover, many representatives are attuned only to organized interests, and do not concern themselves with the unorganized poor.

The connection between voters and their representatives is determined partly by the representative's view of his role. Studies of legislators at the state and national level have found it useful to distinguish three different roles played by legislators: trustee, politico or delegate. Studies of Congress indicate that the politico role is dominant, trustee second, then delegate.[26] Studies of state legislatures show a greater degree of trustee orientation, with politico second.[27] Trustees rely on their own information or consciences in deciding how to vote on public policy, whereas delegates consult their constituent's wishes (or their own understanding of those constituent wishes), and politicos combine the two. Either way, the dominant values of white, middle-class, middle-aged America tend to be the basis for public attempts to deal with the poor.

Even those representatives who are oriented to a delegate function give more attention to the wishes of their more effective constituents—a group whose characteristics and interests diverge markedly from those of the poor. Moreover, they frequently do not reflect the true wishes of their constituency, but their own personal understanding of those wishes. Often representatives define their constituency to a considerable degree in terms of their own life experience.[28]

If representatives are oriented toward a trustee role, the interests of the poor are even less likely to be considered, as the characteristics of representatives are even further divorced from those of the poor than are those of the electorate. Studies have found that "governmental offices are class ranked—the more important the office, the higher the social status of its normal incumbent."[29] Those in a higher socio-economic status basically have more money and access to even more for campaigns, have more leisure and more flexible work schedules, enabling them to campaign, and are more politically aware and likely to possess the relevant skills for a political career. Thus, the "typical" member of the United States Senate since World War II, has been a late middle-aged or elderly, white, Anglo-Saxon, Protestant, native born, lawyer with upper middle-class, rural or small town origins.[30] Similar findings are reported in studies of state legislators: "the lawyer is representative for all population groups—our professional representor; and that part of our population which under any definition, could be called the industrial proletariat enjoys very little membership."³¹ Naturally, those poor below the proletariat level receive none. Thus, whatever the role orientation of representatives, the dominant values of white, upper middle-class, middle-aged America tend to be the basis for public attempts to deal with the poor. In short, the great limitation of the traditional system of American politics is that:

It allows injustices to be inflicted upon those who cannot readily introduce their interests into the political system. Since it depends upon the interaction of "groups with different interests," those people who do not recognize the interests they share with others, who cannot act as a group, and who have little power to make conflicting groups compromise—those people are subject to, rather than participants in, the political order.³²

MULTIPLE DECISION-MAKING CENTERS

American government has been structured so that both *organization and persistence* are needed for groups to have an impact on public policy. Since the poor have lacked the necessary resources and skills for political participation, they have generally been left out of the decision-making process on public policy affecting them.

Paradoxically, the American governmental structure has proved to be both flexible and conservative. Decision making has been decentralized through the dual impact of federalism and the provision of separate institutions sharing power. Thus, federalism has created multiple decision-making centers by making fifty state governments in which public policy is formulated and administered, as well as the national and myriad local governments. Moreover, in *each* government (national, state and local), power is shared by separate institutions—executives, legislatures (usually bicameral), judges and bureaucrats. *Each* of these institutions in *each* of these governments has a *different constituency*. For example, the constituency of a President is national, United States Senators and Governors have statewide constituencies, Congressmen have congressional districts, and the district lines of state legislators are drawn differently from those of Congressmen. Even when the constituency is similar, as with United States Senators and Governors, they are elected on different issues partially because their terms in office differ. Governors serve for two- or four-year terms and about half the state constitutions prohibit election for more than one or two terms; United States Senators may be elected indefinitely for terms of six years. The constituencies of the bureaucracies are highly specialized, and move these decision makers on still different lines.

This multiplicity of decision-making centers means that most organized groups can gain a hearing and influence public policy at some point, which creates a flexible political system in terms of the variety of interests that it can accommodate. However, it also is conservative because of the variety of decision-making centers which can provide more points from which groups can veto the policy initiatives of others. Comprehensive innovation is therefore difficult because so many decision-making centers must be coordinated. The government is so structured that it enables groups to protect their interests by limiting each other's initiatives, thereby protecting the *status quo* which is preferable for them. However, for those who have been left out of the system, such as the poor or racial minorities, comprehensive innovation is needed to create a system from which they themselves can benefit. Since these groups lack either the majorities or established access necessary to protect and advance their interests, the system cannot accommodate them. As a result, after 1965, some advocates of radical restructuring of American values and institutions increasingly turned to violence in an attempt to destroy the system which totally frustrated their need for change.

Beside its protection of the *status quo*, such a decentralized political system results in a decision-making process in which many key questions are the result of non-decision. For example, urban decay was not planned by a power elite. Rather, it resulted from individual pursuit of immediate economic interest at the expense of any coordination or long-range consideration. This situation has been described as one in which:

The most significant fact about the distribution of power in America is not who makes such decisions as are made, but rather, how many matters of the greatest social importance are not objects of anyone's decision at all.[33]

INCREASINGLY PROFESSIONALIZED BUREAUCRACY

There are two basic approaches to integrating public policy: functional and geographic. When done functionally, agencies and personnel at the national, state and local levels sharing the same functional orientation coordinate their efforts. A case in point: functional integration of educational policy would require coordination of the United States Office of Education, state departments of education and local boards of education.

When public policy is integrated geographically, the varied agencies and personnel in a given geographic area coordinate their efforts. Thus, state or local public policy would require the coordination within that geographic area of educational policy with job training and placement policy, welfare policy, police policy, and others.

The geographic approach allows access to elected officials, thereby potentially to the influence of popular majorites. The functional approach emphasizes professionalization in the administration of public policy, leading to bureaucratic autonomy from popular majorities and their elected representatives.

America has already experienced a growing trend toward professionalization in the administration of public policy which has increased the problems of the poor. Increasingly, the administrative bureaucracy has been recruited with specialized perspectives and has therefore been attentive to different groups than have elected representatives. By forming "cozy little triangles" with specialized legislative committees and organized interest groups, the bureaucracy has attempted to restrict policy formulation to these "specialists."[34] Thus, in fields such as education, health and welfare, these professional "experts" have protected their specialized interests against those of the general public. This process has conferred tremendous advantages on established groups and existing ways of doing things. Thus, it has protected the well-organized and well-financed interest groups in each policy area, while strongly deterring a change in the *status quo*.

Educational policy in America, for example, at the present time is functionally integrated, so policy is controlled by a decentralized educational elite that excludes the general public. Three interacting groups, working together to develop and support educational orthodoxy form a nicely closed system for its members. State Education Departments set standards for teacher certification, thereby limiting entry to the profession to those who have been imbued with orthodox approaches. By designating which courses are necessary for certification they develop a community of interest with the Schools of Education, whose function is to transmit the educational orthodoxy. Any that are too innovative discover that their students cannot meet certification requirements. The National Educational Association and its state affiliates are the principal lobbyists for educational policies. Membership is composed of teachers (who have been certified for demonstrating their understanding of the educational orthodoxy) and administrators who must rise through the ranks from the teaching profession. On the ground that they are experts, this combination of bureaucrats and interest groups works together to develop and support orthodox policies for curriculum and internal administrative practices. Because they are well distributed, with centers in every local community, and have access to auxiliary groups such as Parent Teacher Associations, they are politically very effective. Therefore, they are in a good position to form a liaison with members of standing legislative committees on educational policy and to limit local school boards to episodic intervention, without disturbing the fundamental curriculum and administrative practices. The combination of bureaucrats and interest groups to which legislative committeemen have been added forms a closed triangle which an executive can only break with great difficulty, if at all. Consequently, major educational innovation—the Master Teaching Program, Teacher Corps, or incentive pay based on teaching effectiveness—is extremely difficult.

To the degree that the professional bureaucracy is autonomous, its orientation can turn from performance to self-perpetuation: failure of a program becomes less relevant than its own perpetuation. Moreover, the consequence of growing professionalization has barred the public from two crucial areas—the point at which problems are first defined and the point of accountability.[35] The implications of this trend for the poor are obvious: the greater the degree of functional integration the harder it will be for the unorganized to be heard over large, effective economic lobbies.

POLITICAL RESOURCES AND OPPORTUNITIES OF THE POOR

It is clear, then, that the political resources and opportunities available to the poor are extremely limited as a result of their own handicaps and the greater capacity for organization and effectiveness of others. However, there are some differences among the poor themselves as Table 5.3 shows.

In comparing the aged with urban and rural poor, the aged vie with the latter for the dubious honor of having the fewest political resources. Besides being dispersed in the general population and having little organization, the aged are incapacitated for political activism by age and illness ("tea and toast geriatrics"). Both the generation gap and mutual racism make it difficult for them to join other poor groups,

Table 5.3

COMPARISON BY GROUP OF THE AVAILABILITY OF SOME
POLITICAL RESOURCES FOR THE POOR

	GENERAL DIFFERENCES		
	Aged	*Rural poor*	*Urban poor*
Concentration	dispersed	highly dispersed	concentrated
Organization for change	little	little and more dispersed	more extensive and better coordinated
Racial homogeneity	high (85% white)	low: white, Black, Mexican-American, Indian, and some Puerto Rican	low: white, Black, Mexican-American, Puerto Rican, Chinese-American

Table 5.3 (continued)

COMPARISON BY GROUP OF THE AVAILABILITY OF SOME POLITICAL RESOURCES FOR THE POOR

RURAL POOR

	White	Black	Mexican-American	Indian	Migrants
numbers	large but dispersed	less, but concentrated in South	less, but concentrated in Southwest	few and dispersed	few and dispersed
Organization for change	very little	some and increasing	little but increasing	some	little but increasing
Language barrier	no	no	yes	yes	for Mexican-Americans and Puerto Ricans
Racial barriers	no	yes	yes	yes	Yes for all but the small percentage of whites

URBAN POOR

	White	Black	Mexican-American	Puerto Rican	Chinese-American
numbers	large	large	less, but geographically concentrated	even less, but even more highly concentrated	few but highly concentrated
Organization for change	little	considerable and increasing	some and increasing	some and increasing	little and increasing slowly
Language barrier	no	no	yes	yes	yes
Racial barrier	no	yes	yes	yes	yes

and 85 percent of the aged poor are white.[36] Furthermore, many who are former members of the middle class, reduced to poverty by age and illness, are quiet and invisible ("genteel" poverty). Their only asset is public sympathy. There is greater (though hardly high) public willingness to help them than the urban and rural poor, but the public provides subsistence to keep them out of sight.

The rural poor have very few political resources due to both geographic dispersal and the personalistic government (patron system) used in their areas. Migrant farm workers are the most disadvantaged. Lacking even the possibility of a vote, they are people without a country, and language barriers have limited rural Mexican-Americans from effective political organization.[37] Southern blacks, who were influenced by the civil rights movement of the early 1960s, have the asset of group identity which might be a base for political development among the young. Whites have the major advantage in that their problem is entirely economic, without the addition of racial discrimination. Moreover, they often have kinship ties that provide some access to political decision makers. If sufficient government action were taken to change the economic factors affecting them or to create new conditions—job training or development of new industries—their condition could be substantially changed. However, no such action is likely without sustained pressure, which is almost impossible because of their lack of social organization that is caused by their geographic dispersal. They also lack natural leaders because the absence of racial discrimination enables those who are brighter, better educated or more ambitious to move away to find a place in the larger society. Thus, it is from urban poor that major pressures for change must come.

The urban poor benefit from physical concentration, which provides greater communication and mobilization. Also, the broader tax base of urban areas provides better (though still inadequate) services, especially education, transportation and health services. But, they receive less representation than might be expected from their numbers and greater organization due to factors previously discussed, and shifts in election rules during the past decade which have been so structured that they militate against the poor. One technique that has been applied effectively to limit the impact of growing racial minorities in central cities has been the shift from smaller to more inclusive districts. For example, states have shifted to county-wide election of state legislative delegates following a rise in black voting in the central cities.[38] Frequently, a shift from local representation to at-large elections of city councilmen has occurred. The consequence of extending the area of representation, as Madison pointed out in Federalist Paper number Ten, is to dilute the impact of minorities. Another similar recent change has been the shift from partisan to non-partisan elections in many localities, which reduces lower-class mobilization as they are more dependent on cues provided by political parties.[39] Every time blacks get across the minefield to the forest, it seems that whites find a way to move the trees.

Among the urban poor, the displaced rural whites are least likely to organize because of their weakness and small numbers. Also, mutual racism cuts them off from their natural nonwhite economic allies, thereby preventing the development of group identity among the poor—the basis needed for organization—their dilemma since the end of the Populist movement at the close of the nineteenth century.

Puerto Ricans, Mexican-Americans and Chinese-Americans are limited by cultural, racial and language barriers, and those who have not been educated in America lack understanding of the political system. None of these handicaps, though, except racism, affect the urban black poor, who are the most advantaged group of all those that comprise the American poor. Racism has created the ironic advantage of ghettoizing blacks indiscriminately. Their natural leaders, therefore, cannot escape as whites can, giving them a leadership core which made possible both the civil rights movement of the early 1960s and the black power movement that followed. Urbanized Mexican-Americans and Puerto-Ricans share this one ironic advantage of racial segregation so they, too, have an available leadership core. But black organization has been more effective because of their larger numbers and the absence of the language barrier that handicaps the two Spanish-speaking groups.

Even when men exercise the vote, however, it may not change their lives. As a study of the impact of black voting has indicated, the vote is more useful in achieving legal rather than social equality:

. . . the formal mechanisms of democracy do not assure much more than that elites will have incentives to meet demands that do not conflict with the values of the elites and of the majority of the voters. The prospects that votes will help eliminate basic inequalities in the life chances of Negroes are contingent on the degree to which appropriate programs fit within the value structure of elites and voting majorities.

. . . The most frustrating problem of the American Negro in politics is that even if elected policy-makers were totally responsive to Negro demands, it is not at all clear that they have it in their power to eliminate the inequality with which three and a half centuries of discrimination have saddled the American Negro.[40]

Notes

1. GABRIEL KOLKO, *Wealth and Power in America* (New York: Praeger, 1967), p. 45.

2. MICHAEL D. REAGAN, *The Managed Economy* (New York: Oxford University Press, 1967), pp. 8, 76.

3. MORTON GRODZINS, *The American System* (Chicago: Rand McNally, 1966), chap. 14; "Unrepresented Negro Farmers in the South," *The New Republic* (December 25, 1965), 8–9.

4. FAY BENNETT, "The Condition of Farm Workers and Small Farmers in 1969," Report to the National Board of National Sharecropper's Fund (1969), p. 2.

5. GARCEAU, *The Political Life of the American Medical Association.*

6. KOLKO, *Wealth and Power in America*, p. 86.

7. *The Washington Post*, July 15, 1968, B1:1.

8. On the impact of the "joy" drill see Caudill, *Night Comes to the Cumberlands.*

9. *The New York Times*, March 23, 1969, 66:1.

10. *Social Policy*, 1 (May/June, 1970), 7.

11. OSCAR HANDLIN, *The Newcomers* (Garden City, N. Y.: Doubleday, 1962).

12. CHARLES C. KILLINGSWORTH of the University of Michigan, reported in *The New York Times*, April 19, 1970, 4E:7.

13. MANCUR OLSON, *The Logic of Collective Action* (Cambridge, Mass.: Harvard University Press, 1965).

14. *Ibid.*, p. 127.

15. E. E. SCHATTSCHNEIDER, *The Semi-Sovereign People* (New York: Holt, Rinehart & Winston, 1960), p. 35.

16. STANLEY KELLEY, RICHARD AYRES and WILLIAM BOWEN, "Registration and Voting: Putting First Things First," *The American Political Science Review*, 61 (June, 1967), 359–379.

17. CAMPBELL, *et. al.*, p. 283. These findings are supported by subsequent research of which a recent example is DAN NIMMO and CLIFTON McCLESKEY, "Impact of the Poll Tax on Voter Participation: The Houston Metropolitan Area in 1966," *The Journal of Politics*, 31 (August 1969), pp. 682–699.

125

18. *Ibid.*, chap. 17.

19. *Ibid.*, Table 17–4, "Relation of Education to Sense of Political Efficacy, by Region, 1956," p. 479; Table 17–5, "Relation of Education to Sense of Citizen Duty, by Region, 1956," p. 480; Table 17–6, "Relation of Involvement, Efficacy and Education to Vote Turnout. Outside the South, 1956," p. 481.

20. DAVID B. TRUMAN, *The Governmental Process* (New York: Alfred A. Knopf, 1951).

21. *The New York Times*, December 11, 1968, 29:2.

22. AUSTIN RANNEY and LEON D. EPSTEIN, "The Two Electorates: Voters and Non-Voting in a Wisconsin Primary," *The Journal of Politics*, 28 (August 1966), 598–616; AUSTIN RANNEY, "The Representativeness of Primary Electorates," *Midwest Journal of Political Science*, 12 (May 1968), 224–238.

23. Analysis of the Goldwater/Johnson campaign of 1964 supports these findings. No higher level of issue conceptualization on the basis of ideology was found here. PHILIP CONVERSE, AAGE CLAUSEN, WARREN MILLER, "Electoral Myth and Reality: the 1964 Election," *The American Political Science Review*, 59 (June 1965), 321–336.

24. CAMPBELL, *et al.*, Table 10–1, p. 249.

25. *Ibid.*, p. 240.

26. ROGER H. DAVIDSON, *The Role of Congressmen* (New York: Pegasus, 1969), p. 117.

27. HEINZ EULAU, "The Legislator as Representative: Representational Roles," in JOHN C. WAHLKE, HEINZ EULAU, WILLIAM BUCHANAN and LE ROY FERGUSON, eds., *The Legislative System* (New York: John Wiley & Sons, 1962).

28. LEWIS A. DEXTER, "The Representative and His District," *Human Organization*, 16 (1957), 2–13; JOHN W. KINGDON, "Politician's Beliefs About Voters," *The American Political Science Review*, 59 (March 1967), 137–145.

29. DONALD R. MATTHEWS, *United States Senators and Their World* (Chapel Hill, N.C.: University of North Carolina Press, 1960), pp. 44–45.

30. *Ibid.*, p. 44.

31. CHARLES S. HYNEMAN, "Who Makes Our Laws?" in JOHN C. WAHLKE and HEINZ EULAU, eds., *Legislative Behavior* (Glencoe, Ill.: Free Press, 1959), pp. 257–258.

32. JAMES FINN, *Protest, Pacifism and Politics* (New York: Random House, 1968), p. 506.

33. ROBERT WOLFF, *The Poverty of Liberalism* (Boston: Beacon Press, 1968), p. 118.

34. The concept of "cozy little triangles" and its impact on national policies is further discussed in DOROTHY B. JAMES, *The Contemporary Presidency* (New York: Pegasus, 1969). Similar conditions occur on state and local levels.

35. THEODORE LOWI, "The Public Philosophy: Interest-Group Liberalism," *The American Political Science Review*, 61 (March 1967), 5–24.

36. C.E.D. Report, p. 26.

37. SAMORA, *La Raza*.

38. ROYCE HANSON, *The Political Thicket* (Englewood Cliffs, N. J.: Prentice-Hall, Inc., 1966), p. 38. For example, proposal in Georgia legislature to merge Fulton County and Atlanta to dilute the impact of black voting, reported in *The New York Times*, November 9, 1969, 65:1.

39. CHARLES R. ADRIAN, "Some General Characteristics of Non-partisan Elections," *American Political Science Review*, 46 (September 1952), 766–776; ROBERT R. ALFORD and EUGENE C. LEE, "Voting Turnout in American Cities," *American Political Science Review*, 62 (September 1968) 796–813.

40. WILLIAM R. KEECH, *The Impact of Negro Voting* (Chicago: Rand McNally, 1968), pp. 108–109.

SIX

The Cost of American Poverty

Initial costs of poverty are personal and borne by those who are poor, but ultimately it is costly for all members of society. Personally it can hinder both physical and psychological development. To clarify: poverty leads to a high incidence of brain damage which can never be reversed. Disease, hunger and poor nutrition of the mother during the reproductive cycle, and of the child after birth, and environmental hazards are among its causes. Poverty destroys family life because a poor family cannot protect its members—the family's primary purpose. People need interaction in a stimulating environment for full human development, and poverty excludes people from such an environment.[1] As established, American attitudes toward the poor harm their children as students, because they gain a sense of inferiority from the values that dominate their environment.[2] This further blocks self development. In a culture that values materialistic individualism, a man's incapacity to earn a decent wage can destroy his self-respect and hinder his capacity adequately to fulfill his roles as husband and father.

Such handicaps are vastly magnified for the nonwhite poor, who are damaged by racism as well as by the general attitudes toward the poor.[3] The impoverished nature of the life of the poor, particularly nonwhites, is evidenced in many studies by the indices of social pathology. For example, in comparing central Harlem to New York City as a whole, one study finds that:

juvenile delinquency is twice that of the city, habitual narcotics use three to eight times more; venereal disease among youth is six times more; infant mor-

128

tality is double; homicide rate six times more; Aid to Dependent Children supports three times as many youths under 18.[4]

Poverty is also costly in social terms, because society cannot benefit from the undeveloped capacities and talents of poor people. Their low productivity results in a lower standard of living for all citizens than is necessary.[5] Thus, having persons in a poverty status is economically wasteful for an entire society. Furthermore, there are high costs to a nation in the tensions, chaos and dislocations that lead to heavy expenditures on police protection, court and prison systems, mental hospitals and emergency wards.[6]

CULTURE VS. CLASS

Analysts of poverty tend to divide between those who ascribe the behavior of poor people to distinctive cultural patterns and those who consider it a reflection of social class. A "culture of poverty" has been defined by anthropologist Oscar Lewis as having:

its own structure and rationale, as a way of life that is passed down from generation to generation along family lines. . . . the culture of poverty in modern nations is not only a matter of economic deprivation, of disorganization or of the absence of something. It is also something positive and provides some rewards without which the poor could hardly carry on.[7]

Because Oscar Lewis' work was far more complex and subtle than that of other writers who used some form of the concept of "culture of poverty,"[8] much of the criticism of the concept is more relevant to their work than to his. However, even he did not escape some serious problems in using it. For example, his focus on it as a defense mechanism undercut his own argument—to the degree that the behavior of poor people is defensive, it is not autonomous. Rather, it is integrally related to the values of the larger society.

Advocates of the "culture of poverty" explanation assume that poor people have a set of values distinct from those of the middle class, which they judge (whether explicitly or implicitly) to be inherently inferior. Even Oscar Lewis' romanticization of the poor entailed some condescension—hence some hidden condemnation—but most advocates are much more openly hostile to the poor than was Lewis.

In contrast, those who ascribe the behavior of poor people to social class suggest that the poor do not have a distinctive set of values. Rather, their behavior reflects adaptations developed as an expedient after failure to realize the behavior patterns demanded by middle-class society. The failure is not personal, but the result of economic, social and political barriers.[9]

These two approaches differ substantially in their implications for social change. If poverty forms a distinctive "culture," then change can only come from the poor themselves. Thus such a concept is highly protective of the *status quo*—if the poor are culturally different from the rest of us there is little or nothing we can do for them. So, we have a 20th-century version of the old liberal and Calvinist ascription of poverty to personal failure. Rather than discussing the persistence of poverty in moralistic terms, it is considered in sophisticated anthropological ones that replace personal failure with the explanation of a subculture that is maladaptive for change. The net result, however, is the same—the Lord (or society) can only care for those who help themselves.

However, if failure is not personal, but the result of economic, social and political barriers, it could be altered by public policy designed to remove such barriers. In short, in order to alleviate poverty, those who ascribe the behavior of the poor to a distinctive culture require the poor to change themselves, whereas those who ascribe the behavior of the poor to their position as the bottom stratum in a highly stratified society require change in the institutions of that society.

In American terms, the concept of the culture of poverty had particular significance during the 1960s, as it became the basis for public policy toward the poor, reflected in such programs as the War on Poverty. The speed with which this concept was widely disseminated and accepted may be partially attributed to the ease with which its implicit assumptions fit into existing middle-class stereotypes and preferences. Naturally, however, it was presented as the fruits of "objective," "value-free" scholarship.

The degree to which adherents of the concept of a "culture of poverty" were actually being *subjective* was demonstrated by Charles A. Valentine through a concise analysis of the writings of a half-dozen leading advocates of the position. He found that their work essentially constituted "prejudgments of empirical questions,"[10] and that: "Most of the putative culture patterns ascribed to the lower-class poor by [those] writers . . . have a quality of hyperbole and simplification."[11]

For example, Nathan Glazer and Daniel Moynihan were found by Valentine to have indulged in "sweeping generalizations, invidious comparisons, and harsh value-judgments . . . in the absence of concrete knowledge or experience of the shape and dynamics of ongoing social existence."[12] Thus, Moynihan's report on appropriate public policy for the Negro family resolved itself "into a strategy for strengthening existing centers of power and privilege, offered to the affluent so that they may preserve their advantages against a threat from the poor."[13]

Valentine found that Oscar Lewis' methodology led to inconsistencies between his abstractions and the data on which they were based that undercut their validity. In sum, this analysis found that a "culture of poverty" had never been proven by its promoters. Consequently, it should never have been the basis of public policy.

The bulk of social science research over the past decade has provided data supportive of class rather than culture as an explanation of the behavior of poor people.[14] Thus, the vast body of literature indicates that the poor *are* different, but that their differences appear mainly to be a matter of degree rather than of kind:

> If there is a culture of poverty or a subculture of the poor, then it is a condition that arises out of the exigencies of being relatively without resources, and of being negatively evaluated by the larger society. Furthermore, if there is a culture or a subculture of poverty only in this limited sense, then it is not clear what is gained, except dramatic emphasis, by the use of the term.[15]

A brief consideration of the work of five representative scholars suggests the validity of this conclusion. For example, Roger Hurley found that: "Life in the Central Ward in Newark is primitive; the needs of its inhabitants are primary; and its people are as isolated and as vulnerable as the unarmed infantryman in the Vietnamese jungle."[16] He found that this condition resulted far less from their personal inadequacies than from the total inadequacy of economic, social, health, educational and welfare institutions. Rather than assisting the poor, Hurley found that in Newark these institutions further reinforced their deprivation, and functioned to maintain them in poverty.

Similarly, Gerald Suttles' analysis of three years as a participant observer in the Addams area on the Near West Side of Chicago supported a class interpretation of the behavior of the poor. Since the Addams area was a multi-ethnic slum community of Italians, blacks, Mexicans and Puerto Ricans, he was able to compare the norms and practices of these four groups with each other, as well as with those of the larger American society. He found that the slum neighborhood did, in fact, have a set of behavior standards different from the larger society, but that this in no way constituted a distinct "culture of poverty." Rather, he found that these poor people aspired to conventional norms that could not be met in that particular environment, and therefore:

Conventional norms are not rejected but differentially emphasized or suspended for established reasons. The vast majority of the residents are quite conventional people. . . . Neither disorganization nor value rejection are apt terms to describe the Addams area. Certainly the social practices of the residents are not just an inversion of those of the wider society, and the inhabitants would be outraged to hear as much. Also, the neighborhood is not a cultural island with its own distinct and imported traditions.[17]

While many of the social arrangements of the Addams area might seem to be a denial of the norms of the larger society, if taken out of context, he found that as a whole: "the residents are bent on ordering local relations where the beliefs and evaluations of the wider society do not provide adequate guidelines for conduct."[18] To reach this conclusion Suttles analyzed the institutions (religion, commercial exchanges, recreation and education), patterns of communication (language, gestures, clothing, grooming and personal display), and communication channels of the Addams area, the function of ethnic solidarity and the socialization process undergone by boys there. He concluded that:

The subculture of the Addams area is more nearly a means of gradually discovering a moral order than a set of rules which one mechanically obeys.[19]
   The moral order created by Addams area residents does not meet either their own ideals or those of the wider society. The local people recognize as much and view their way of life as a practical exigency.[20]

Elliott Lebow's study of black streetcorner men in Washington, D. C., came to a similar conclusion. He found that:

the streetcorner man does not appear as a carrier of an independent cultural tradition. His behavior appears not so much as a way of realizing the distinctive goals and values of his own subculture, or of conforming to its models, but rather as his way of trying to achieve many of the goals and values of the larger society, of failing to do this, and of concealing his failure from others and from himself as best he can.[21]

The "culture of poverty" argument was further undercut by Otis Dudley Duncan, based on a sophisticated statistical analysis of the relation between family origin and poverty for blacks, and the relation between their school scores and poverty.[22] His statistical model demonstrated that for blacks, race was a more important determinant of poverty than the socio-economic origins of parents, and that differences in school scores could only explain a small part of the occupation and income differences between blacks and whites. Thus, he proved that blacks in America have not been poor because they have come from a distinctive "culture," but because of the pervasive racial discrimination that they have faced.
   As a final example of recent research, Lee Rainwater found that a "culture of poverty" concept was not adequate to explain data from a St. Louis housing project. Rather, he found that: "conventional society man-

ages somehow to inculcate its norms even in those persons who are not able to achieve successfully in terms of them and to prevent any efforts to redefine norms within the lower-class subculture in such a way that contrary views acquire full normative status."[23] Thus, Rainwater maintained that any distinctive elements of a lower-class subculture merely represented adaptive behavior on the part of persons who had been disinherited by their society.[24]

In summary, on the basis of various research and statistical techniques there is a general scholarly concensus that American poverty has *not* been the result of a distinctive cultural pattern generationally transmitted.

Lengthy statistics and studies are vehicles which indicate the impact of poverty on the poor and the problems in dealing with it, but actual life experiences make the point best. These are real people, who directly face the costs of American poverty, but their names and some details have been changed to protect their privacy. Their experiences clearly reveal that their poverty is not solely a consequence of personal failure or a distinctive value pattern.

BESSIE SMITH: WOMEN'S WORK . . .

Bessie Smith was born in 1915, in the quiet rural backwater of Saint Helena Parrish, Louisiana, fourth of seven children of a tenant farmer. So many rural depressions had affected the South during her parents' lives that 1929 occasioned no particular notice at first. Eventually, however, credit dried up, there was no market for crops, therefore, no cash to replace broken equipment or buy the necessities they could not produce. Barter worked for a while, but their white land owner began to demand cash payments rather than a portion of crops from the tenants on his land. To earn it, the family broke up, leaving the parents and three younger children to tend the farm while the four eldest sought work in the cities.

Bessie and her older sister went to New Orleans to become domestics. There she met Leroy Smith, a cook on a merchant vessel whose home port was Long Beach, California. Of necessity, their courtship was brief. After a very simple wedding ceremony Leroy sailed back to Long Beach to await her while Bessie began married life with a solitary trip across the country.

The ghetto life of Watts was harsh, but there were few other places in Los Angeles where a black couple could rent an apartment then. Leroy was gone a lot, leaving Bessie to adjust as best she could without friends, family or a job. Tension mounted between them, until the birth of a daughter, Della, which seemed to bring new happiness. Then Leroy lost his job. There were few jobs during the Depression, especially for blacks, who were traditionally "last hired, first fired." Because the flood of poor white "Oakies" to California absorbed all the unskilled agricultural jobs, and he could find no work in Los Angeles, his anger and frustration mounted. When Bessie had to return to domestic work to support them he turned to drink. Finally, he could no longer cope with the situation and left her.

Meanwhile, Bessie's father had died, and the younger children went to live with relatives, so Bessie sent what she could borrow from employers to her mother to come West and care for Della while Bessie worked hard. Once Della was in school Bessie's mother tried to work as a domestic, but her health failed. Since both women feared the influence of Watts on Della if she were left alone, it was agreed that Bessie should remain their sole support. Over the years the two women managed to cope with their hardships and encouraged Della to study and make something of herself.

Eventually, Della became a dietician, was married shortly after and moved to New York, where she bore two children. Bessie was proud of Della's happy marriage and her grandsons, but her financial load remained heavy. When a sister and her husband were killed in an automobile accident, their son came West to live with Bessie and her ailing mother. The boy proved much harder to raise than had Della.

Despite real affection for them, he was restive in a world of simple, pious older women. For relief he turned to the male world of the streets. At first this caused no problem in his school work, as he was exceptionally bright and able to handle his lessons with little effort. His high school guidance counselor informed Bessie that he had a genius I.Q. and that he should be encouraged to go to college, but teachers and lessons seemed increasingly irrelevant to the world he knew on the streets. He began to skip classes to spend more time with his friends experimenting with drugs.

It was easy to hide this from Bessie. Her hours were long and the work very tiring. Her nephew was still asleep at five-thirty when she left to catch the infrequent bus from Watts that connected with a Los Angeles bus. Public transportation from Watts was so inadequate that it took two hours to reach employers that she could have reached in a half hour by car. But a car was a luxury Bessie could not afford, so six days a week she was away from home for fourteen hours, four of which were spent riding buses. She returned after seven, often too tired to eat. Increasing dizzy spells had troubled her for some time, but there were more pressing problems with which to cope. Her mother's faculties were deteriorating, leaving her oblivious to the world around her and in need of constant care.

When Bessie had taken her to the public health clinic one time their apartment was burglarized. The thieves took almost every possession that Bessie had accumulated over a frugal lifetime. Naturally, the thieves were never found, and everything was a complete loss since no insurance company would issue a policy to a poor slum dweller. Bessie wanted to move, but an income of $60 a week for three people left little for additional rent. Although over thirty years had elapsed since coming to Los Angeles, as a black she still found it hard to rent housing outside the ghetto. With all these problems, it took some time before Bessie became aware of her nephew's truancy—not until she was summoned to school to explain it. This was the first of many encounters and the first of many work days Bessie would miss on his account.

When the federal government began an intensive campaign to shut off the supply of marijuana, users turned to heroin. Like teenagers elsewhere, Bessie's nephew felt that he would never be "hooked," and like others he, too, became addicted. To support the habit, he and his friends became petty thieves and purse snatchers. Though such activities sickened him, his addiction compelled him to continue.

At the point when her nephew needed her, Bessie was unable to give him attention because of her own accumulating health problems. Medical care had always seemed a luxury for which she had neither money nor time. Everyone she knew feared doctors and hospitals, and accepted aches and pains as unavoidable signs of aging. Though Della's sons thought she was a swinging grandma, Bessie had to admit to herself that the years were taking their toll. The dizzy spells became worse and were accompanied by nausea. A growth on her leg was also troubling her. Finally she went to a clinic which took a whole day because it was in downtown Los Angeles, and was open only in the daytime. The staff gave her tests and examined her, to find cancerous growths on her leg and in her womb. Surgery was needed, but many accumulated health problems made it impossible. Since her blood sugar level and blood pressure were too high to chance an immediate operation, she returned to Watts with a strict diet and a useless injunction to rest.

An ugly shock awaited her at home. Her nephew had been arrested for hitting an old woman while trying to steal her purse to get money to support his habit. Only Bessie's strong religious faith gave her enough strength in the weeks ahead to find a lawyer, borrow money for his fee and her nephew's bail and appear in court with him. Naturally, this meant missing work and loss of income. This meant that she could not afford the high protein/low carbohydrate diet that had been prescribed. Her blood pressure mounted seriously.

Months passed waiting for the case to come to trial on Los Angeles' crowded court docket, so Bessie returned to work. Her tensions mounted as her mother's health grew worse and her own remained precarious. The added strain of worry over her nephew's case and his daily whereabouts brought on an ulcer.

In treating the ulcer the doctor discovered the need for immediate surgery on the two cancers. She had to stop working and take medication and be on a special diet to bring her blood sugar level down before surgery. Della and her husband helped as much as they could financially, but Bessie was only able to keep a roof over her head by illegally subletting part of her apartment. Her nephew, who by this time had been placed in a reformatory, was unable to help. Meager Social Security payments did not even cover the cost of transportation to the clinic and food for her and her mother. Six months passed before the blood sugar level and blood pressure were low enough to operate. While in the hospital she contracted pneumonia. The possibility of recuperating sufficiently to resume work was very dim for many months, but without work she would have no money for the medicine, food and care needed for recuperation. After a year's absence, her former employers had made other arrangements, so she would have to search for work—a weak, ill, fifty-five-year-old black woman with a year and a half work record of irregularity and absenteeism caused by ill health and personal problems. Previous employers were not enthusiastic about giving references.

JEREMY SHAW: DOWN AND OUT DOWN EAST

A small bent figure thrown into sharp relief against the snow trudged along the edge of the highway. Pausing to shift his forty-pound hemp sack, he blew on cramped fingers showing red through remnants of wool gloves. The sack, wind-whipped cheeks and frost-covered beard gave him a quaint appearance that made Jeremy Shaw seem part of the picturesque Maine landscape to passing cars of skiers. For seventy-five years Jeremy had been more picturesque than self-sufficient in a region that was a tourist haven because of its economic plight. Natural beauty and low prices lured the well-to-do from all over. But for the "natives," Maine had been a depressed area for several generations.

Along that highway all Jeremy could think of was his hunger and reaching home so he could eat. Pains of age, the cold, the long walk and his heavy sack seemed insignificant compared to that primary need. At last a six mile journey was over, as his tarpaper shack came in view. To tourists who happened to notice it, the shack appeared to be a shelter for hunters. For Jeremy the one small room warmed and lit by a kerosene stove with a nearby privy and a frozen pump had been "home" for fifty years.

He opened a can of meat from his sack and wolfed it down without bothering to heat it. Next Jeremy ate a can of vegetables and another of fruit. This monthly banquet over, he stored away the rest of his month's supplies from the federal food distribution plan, and huddling deeper into his worn coat, fell asleep.

Life had fallen into a monthly pattern of desperate hunger, temporarily satisfied by the food distribution. First he ate the canned food, then the items that needed cooking like flour, lard, beans and powdered milk. Inevitably, they disappeared too soon, leaving him with growing hunger in the last week, when he would be waiting for the right day and hour to take the six-mile walk to the local firehouse with a sack as empty as his belly. Eight months a year he froze, and in early June he nearly went mad daily during the black fly season when swarms of black flies viciously bit, to the point of bleeding.

There was little conversation at the firehouse. Beside the town's well polished 1937 fire engine, a dispirited group collected hours before the distribution truck was due to arrive. A mother nursing her infant and fifteen elderly people shared both the firehouse's warmth and a common expectation that their hunger would soon be appeased. No need for talk when they had experienced similar lifetimes of hunger.

Jeremy stood next to William Carter. Since his wife had died of pneumonia, he had lived alone in an old farm house that was falling down around his ears. It had been built in the Victorian boom days and had not been repaired for over a generation. Before the food program he had scavenged refuse at the county dump to survive. Beside him was Thomas Pyle who actually had to live *on* the county dump because he could not afford enough land for his "home"—the body of a truck with a stove pipe stuck in the middle. County health authorities looked the other way since there really was no place for Thomas to go. Jeremy, William and Thomas had always been poor, born into the third generation of poverty. They had never been able to earn enough to have had any savings or Social Security, and they knew that it was useless to leave their home state to seek jobs elsewhere because they had no education or skill.

Sarah Hardy was different. She *had* worked most of her life, but hunger showed in the faded blue eyes beneath her hat of ancient vintage. She was on the food line, despite Social Security. Previously, each month she had received a $40 Social Security check and $20 in state old-age assistance after a lifetime of hard work. In 1970, when the federal government had raised Social Security payments, "economy-minded"

Maine had promptly cut state aid to the elderly, reducing Sarah to a monthly income of $57.

There were many other county residents who were eligible for the food program but were too proud to accept relief. Typical was an elderly, bed-ridden, diabetic woman receiving a monthly Social Security payment of $60, and $19 from the state old-age assistance program. When poverty workers tried to sign her up for the food program, she smiled gamely and said, "One day when I can't hold my head up, I'll come to you."

Annie Pyle looked a couple of decades older than her forty-five years. Unlike most of the others, who worked hard for a clean, neat appearance, she was unabashedly slovenly. She lived with eight filthy children in an unfurnished shack, whose floor, on which they slept and ate, was of moldy garbage. The yard was a sea of garbage. She came from three generations of slovenly women, and knew no better. Her husband was thoroughly shiftless, breaking everything in sight in fits of drunken rage. Their children were stunted physically and mentally, and seemed likely to follow in their parents' footsteps.

Eventually, their vigil was rewarded by the appearance of a rickety truck. A highly improbable figure jumped down, tall, lithe, muscular, a blue beret perched jauntily on black hair just beginning to show traces of grey. George Nalbandian was their lifeline to the world.

GEORGE NALBANDIAN: FROM GENERATIONS OF TURK FIGHTERS

George, known affectionately by his staff as "Grumpy," was a man whose daily life was spent fighting poverty, selfish and short-sighted local communities and legislative and bureaucratic incompetence. The battle was constant, inescapable and wearing. The incredible dedication needed for this food distributor and his staff underscored how difficult it was to get *one* adequate program in a *single* county. In explaining his survival under the pressures, George would simply refer to his Armenian heritage with an expressive shrug, by saying, "I come from generations of Turk fighters." It seemed to take that heritage to cope with the nearly impossible job.

Although the food distribution program was reaching only a third of those eligible in the county, it meant distribution of forty-five tons of food a month at the rate of forty pounds a person. To accomplish such a feat, George and a staff of two women were given equipment and storage facilities that would have been appropriate props for a Mack Sennett comedy. For distributing these tons of food in towns throughout the county each month, facing back-country roads, uncertain weather conditions and a winter that lasted for eight months, $400 had been provided. Poverty dominated the structure of the program as well as being its subject matter.

Their first truck had only one defect—its brakes failed in cold weather. Lacking any way to trade trucks with another food distributor in Florida, George adopted a cold weather battle plan: He would leave the doors open so that he and his assistants could jump out if necessary. Despite the benefits of so much fresh air and exercise, few tears were shed when the truck blew its engine.

The second truck had brakes, so George could leave the doors closed and luxuriate in comparative warmth, but it compensated with a series of minor idiosyncracies that caused him to spend hours under the hood wielding tools and muttering choice Armenian imprecations. A typical day would be spent covering seventy miles of upland, distributing several tons of food at various stops. Lunch was cheese and crackers eaten while driving to meet a tight schedule—hungry people were depending on them. Barring truck problems, they would return to headquarters late in the afternoon to complete forms and do paper work which often seemed to equal the food tonnage. George spent long hours visting homes to check eligibility; and evenings were often spent at community meetings around the county.

Relations with the communities were often strained. Personal squabbles and petty bickering among community members frequently ensued. The selectmen who ran local towns (usually local businessmen) sometimes tried to act as feudal overlords, attempting to exercise control over the choice of those who were to receive aid. Most problems arose from the total blind spots of the middle class to the problems of the poor.

For example, in 1970 ecology and environmental control had become a popular issue among the middle class throughout America. Characteristically, the local chapter of a major national woman's organization attacked the problem with more vigor than foresight. Since the major polluter of rivers in the area was the state's leading electrical power company, they selected a more modest target: a tannery. It was found to be polluting a stream. Since very few people benefitted from the tannery's operation, it was possible to gain popular support for a demand to shut it down. At this point they ran into conflict with George Nalbandian.

The tannery employed 156 men and women, who would not be able to find new jobs in a depressed economy. Including their dependents, about 400 people would be deprived of income merely to satisfy the crusading spirit of a group of clubwomen. When they refused to listen to George's suggestion that they instead compel the plant to install pollution-control devices, rather than closing it entirely, he confronted them with the implications of their action. Outraged, the good ladies accomplished their original goal, and then turned on George.

Since he had to distribute forty-five tons of food a month he needed a large storage space. It had been provided in the basement of the county courthouse. However, after the tannery incident a judge (whose wife was chairman of the club) decided that he needed to have part of the basement remodeled for a special sessions courtroom which would rarely be used. Therefore, the food distribution program was evicted. The only place George could find was an abandoned 1930 aircraft hangar. No words were needed to express his disgust when George stood in the middle of this derelict surveying the gaping holes in the roof, missing wall boards, and doors so warped that a child could crawl through without opening them. Perhaps he was considering the crash helmet and armor he would need to cope with all the cans of food exploding in the first freeze.

JOSÉ GARCIA: REDUNDANT MAN

As a boy José Garcia was brought to New York City from Puerto Rico by his parents, who sought relief from the island's grinding poverty. Growing up in the rough street life of Spanish Harlem, he had become versed beyond his years in human passions, weaknesses and fears.

Initially, José was limited in his studies by having to learn subjects in a foreign tongue. For children of *El Barrio,* English was a language they relegated solely to school. Because Puerto Ricans, like earlier poor immigrants who had come to New York, were economically and ethnically segregated, all of José's family, neighbors and friends spoke Spanish. English was spoken outside *El Barrio,* but children rarely left it except to go to the public health clinic. Within Spanish Harlem only policemen, social workers, teachers or store owners spoke English.

Even if José had not faced a language barrier, the public schools of Spanish Harlem would have offered little encouragement for learning. Classes were so overcrowded that they were held in two shifts daily. Plaster was falling, windows were broken and boarded up against winter winds, the plumbing was so bad that the school smelled constantly from backed-up toilets. There was no equipment for sports, so all that restless boys could do for exercise was to chase rats, squash cockroaches and work off pent up energies by disrupting classes. This behavior so upset a series of young female teachers, fresh out of college and still devoted to writing irrelevant lesson plans, that José's class went through seven in three years with a number of interim substitutes.

Finally, Mr. Harris, an ex-Marine licensed to teach physical education, was assigned to José's class. Order was established quickly after the first show-down in which he beat three boys. Thereafter, order was maintained by Mr. Harris' system of deputizing two class bullies to be "monitors," overlooking their physical brutality against classmates. There was a degree of peace but no learning. José came to hate school because he caught the brunt of much bullying since he was nearly as strong as the monitors and therefore posed a threat to them. To avoid being called a coward by his friends, he faced a daily cut lip, bloody nose or bruises. For José and his classmates, school was a failure.

An indication of the deficiency of his school was proven by the low score it received on standard reading tests administered to students throughout New York City. The students in José's ninth grade class were reading four years behind grade level. José felt little incentive to finish high school, much less continue on to college, so he dropped out.

His first job was as a bowling alley pin setter, but he was fired when automatic pin setters were installed. For a while he washed dishes in a downtown restaurant, but like others, the restaurant replaced men with dishwashing machines. His next job as an elevator operator ended in the same way. Increasingly, there were fewer unskilled jobs.

Meanwhile, José had married, and within four years he had fathered three children. He could hardly afford to be out of work. He managed to find an unskilled job at the General Motors' Tarrytown plant at an unbelievable wage of $2.75 an hour, or $440 a month—over twice the minimum state wage.

By 1970 his family expenses had greatly increased. With the three children attending school, there were constant demands for money. His wife could not work because their second grader went to the morning session, the first grader, afternoons and the Kindergartener spent only three hours a day in school.

By relying heavily on a diet of beans and rice, the five Garcias spent only $40 a week on food. Clothing was passed down from child to child and repaired frequently, but when it wore out there was no money to replace it, or to buy shoes. Furniture and major appliances were needed, but they could not get credit at reputable banks or stores, so a third of their time payments were for exorbitant interest charges for shoddy merchandise. By paying into a car pool José was able to cut travel expenses to Tarrytown. His salary just covered the family's expenses:

Rent	$ 95
Gas and electric	10
Food	160
Drugs and medicine	10
Clothing for five	25

Time payment on furniture and household appliances	25
School expenses for three children	12
Personal items (e.g., haircuts, sanitary & hygienic supplies)	10
Cleaning products, laundry, minimal dry cleaning & shoe repair	12
Subway and bus fares for family (allowing only 2 trips daily)	36
Income tax and Social Security	25
Church collection	5
Car pool	15
Total monthly expenses	$440

This left no money for a telephone, any kind of insurance or other "luxuries" such as vacations, presents, books, magazines, newspapers, entertainment or membership in any group or organization, not even a church group because the Garcias could not afford enough clothes to maintain family pride, or the expected contributions but they survived.

For a year and a half José's life was a pattern of getting up at six, meeting his car pool at seven, and clocking in at the plant at eight. The work was exhausting because he had to run along the conveyor belt between fixed points, trying to finish his assigned operations on each car that passed and get back to the next in time to complete work on it. The monotony often lulled him into a state of mindless action that was dangerous, because men were frequently hurt in the machinery when they were not careful. Often, instead of eating, he fell dead asleep during the half hour lunch break. Then the afternoon seemed endless—an infinite succession of cars with José running between them like a man on a treadmill. At night he sometimes dreamed of it as an infinite process, with the cars growing larger and larger and the treadmill moving faster until he would wake up with sweat on his forehead and a dry throat.

After work, José and five companions would laughingly make the sign of the cross before entrusting their lives to an automobile that had far more past than future. Apparently, 1955 had not been a vintage year for Fords, certainly not for that one. It had gone through a dozen owners before reaching Luis Hernandez for the sum of fifty dollars. That was the last bargain Luis had from the car. Piece by piece it was almost rebuilt from the inside out. Every time one worn-out part was replaced another began its death rattle. The six companions grew accustomed to a regular disaster routine on the route to and from work with assigned jobs like going for help, directing traffic and moving the car onto a siding. It was often vandalized for parts when parked overnight, but no thief was ever blind enough to steal it.

The precarious nature of José's transportation caused him to be late with increasing frequency. At first his supervisor was understanding, but tolerance soon wore thin. His patience snapped the morning after José had not come to work at all. The six friends had seen the end of their transportation the previous morning when their car finally gave up the ghost during rush hour on the Major Deegan Expressway. Only by extraordinary good luck had they escaped serious harm when the axle broke and the car careened into the right hand retaining wall. Next morning all but Ramon, who had received a concussion, took a bus to work. It was twice as expensive as the car pool and twice as long because they first had to take a bus and subway to the bus terminal. If they missed the return bus at five the next one was an hour later.

José's fatigue was so intense that the sounds of three children in a two-room apartment became intolerable. His frustrations mounted as he went through each day of quiet desperation. It seemed as though at least one of the children was always sick, and his wife was always asking for money which he did not have.

His short temper at work hardly won appreciation from his supervisor, who began to ride José constantly. Things went from bad to worse until he finally found himself standing outside the plant gate with two weeks severance pay in his hand and no job.

In *El Barrio*, there were no full-time jobs to be found. Half the men he knew were unemployed, and most of the others could only find part-time work, or work far below the federal minimum wage. Finally, José found a warehouse job that paid $60 a week, but the $240 a month could never meet his family's needs. If he deserted them, Aid to Dependent Children would pay his wife and three children $249.75 a month, from which no taxes would be taken. There would also be separate medical payments equivalent to about $60 a month. In fact, his family would be financially better off without him.

ALICE WHITECLOUD: THE COSTS OF BEING "QUAINT"

For Alice Whitecloud, an eight-year-old Navaho girl, the "scenic Southwest" was a living hell. Of the twelve children her mother had borne, only four had survived infancy. Since she had been a premature baby, weighing only four pounds, her first few months had been spent in a hospital where doctors tried to overcome the effects of malnutrition and to build her resistance.

She had still made a frail bundle when her parents were finally able to take Alice home to one of a cluster of squalid shacks which housed three dozen families in one corner of an Arizona reservation. There was no electricity, sewage or running water. Dust from the rutted street clung to everything, giving clothes, houses and people a faded appearance. Relentlessly, the wind swept sand across the vast, flat expanse of the reservation, bringing bitter cold in winter and parching heat in the summer. During those early years Alice was often ill. The family's steady diet of Navaho fry-bread barely kept them alive. Sometimes there was not even fry-bread.

Her mother's face was deeply lined with age, illness, and care, and she was nearly toothless. Like most others on the reservation she was very fat because of the poor diet, but she was warm and comforting, and had many ways to ease a child's pain or bring her joy. Her father's face was brown and cracked like the earth in summer, but his pride in their people's heritage was a source of strength to the whole family. His eyes would glow and his whole face look younger as he sat by the fire at night telling stories of olden days.

By the age of eight Alice's memories of that life had grown dim. At six she had been taken from the world she knew to a Bureau of Indian Affairs boarding school which was a former isolated army post that had been condemned. A grim external appearance was matched by the charm of its interior decor. Alice's dormitory held forty iron beds and washstands in a row. One attendant was responsible for dressing, washing, housecleaning, and supervising the free time of both the girls' and boys' dorms, which housed seventy children. At night one attendant was responsible for over twice as many.

All individuality in dress was prohibited, as was use of the Navaho language. Instruction in all subjects was entirely in English, taught by people who could not understand the children's language and therefore could not bridge the gap of understanding. Even had the children understood the lessons they would hardly have heard a word about their people's rich heritage, even in the American history class.

The school's attitude that Indians were inferiors whose background should be destroyed showed in every aspect of the regimented day. Every hour was planned, supervised and regulated by the bell schedule, with instructors making frequent head counts to be sure that everyone was present. In changing from one activity to another, the children had to march in squad lines. Communication between them was strongly discouraged. Classes, meals, study periods, chores, free time and bedtime never varied. At eight years Alice could tell exactly what she would be doing most hours of her life for the next eight years. Parent's visits were discouraged; and poverty made other than an occasional weekend at home impossible.

With three other girls Alice had tried to run away several times, but the punishment had been so painful that she was afraid to try again. Children were always running away from school, but never got very far. Older students turned to sniffing airplane glue, or alcohol when they could get it, as a means to escape, but nothing really helped. Despair was so deep that during her two years at the school Alice had seen fifteen of the older students attempt (some succeed in) suicide.

In her "free time" she would sit listlessly looking out at the plains, a sullen, hopeless expression on her face. At eight Alice Whitecloud faced a future of stultifying boredom.

Notes

1. LAWRENCE HAWORTH, "Deprivation and the Good City," in BLOOMBERG & SCHMANDT, eds.
2. GRIER and COBBS, *Black Rage*, p. 132.
3. For a psychological study of the impact of racism on personality structure, see *Ibid.*
4. H.A.R.Y.O.U.,
5. ROBERT J. LAMPMAN, "Income Distribution and Poverty," in GORDON, ed., *Poverty in America.*
6. HARRINGTON, *The Other America.*
7. LEWIS, *LaVida*, p. xliii.
8. For examples of analysis of poverty on the ground that it constitutes a distinctive culture see FRANKLIN FRAZIER, *The Negro Family in the United States* (Chicago: University of Chicago Press, 1966); NATHAN GLAZER and DANIEL P. MOYNIHAN, *Beyond the Melting Pot* (Cambridge, Mass.: Harvard University Press, 1963); DANIEL P. MOYNIHAN, *The Negro Family*; WALTER B. MILLER, "Lower Class Culture as a Generalizing Milieu of Gang Delinquency," *Journal of Social Issues*, 14 (1965), 5–19; DAVID MATZA, "The Disreputable Poor," NEIL SMELSER and SEYMOUR M. LIPSET, eds. *Social Structure and Mobility in Economic Development*, (Chicago: Aldine, 1966).
9. American writers who use this approach include KENNETH CLARK, *Dark Ghetto*; THOMAS GLADWIN, *Poverty U. S. A.*; ELLIOTT LEBOW, *Tally's Corner: A Study of Negro Streetcorner Men* (Boston: Little, Brown, 1967).
10. CHARLES A. VALENTINE, *Culture and Poverty* (Chicago: University of Chicago Press, 1970), p. 16.
11. *Ibid.*, p. 43.
12. *Ibid.*, p. 27.
13. *Ibid.*, p. 42.
14. A content analysis of poverty literature finds this pattern of concensus: PETER ROSSI and ZAHAVIA BLUM, "Class, Status and Poverty," DANIEL P. MOYNIHAN, ed., *On Understanding Poverty* (New York: Basic Books, 1969).

15. *Ibid.*, pp. 56–57.

16. HURLEY, *Poverty and Mental Retardation*, p. 197.

17. SUTTLES, *The Social Order of the Slum.*

18. *Ibid.*, p. 4.

19. *Ibid.*, p. 233.

20. *Ibid.*, p. 234.

21. LEBOW, *Tally's Corner*, p. 222.

22. OTIS DUDLEY DUNCAN, "Inheritance of Poverty or Inheritance of Race?", MOY-NIHAN, ed., *On Understanding Poverty.*

23. LEE RAINWATER, "The Problems of Lower-Class Culture and Poverty War Strategy," in *Ibid.*, p. 244.

24. *Ibid.*, p. 247.

SEVEN

The Chances for Change

How likely is the American political system to pay more for less poverty; and how likely is it that willingness to pay more will result in less poverty, given the impediments involved? *Some* change is possible but the degree to which an individual will consider such change significant will depend upon his initial definition of poverty, which is related to personal value choices.

To believers in the tenets of utilitarian liberalism (American "conservatives") poverty is defined in subsistence terms but it is not legitimately the object of major public-policy initiatives. Consequently, they maintain that the political system should not pay more to alleviate it. Since this group constitutes a large minority of the population it has sufficient access to and influence upon elected and appointed officials to slow the speed of change and limit its scope.

To believers in the tenets of various versions of socialism, only a thorough-going restructuring of American economic, social and political institutions would be acceptable, since they define poverty in terms of the relative distribution of wealth in a society. Throughout American history there have been a small number of advocates of just such profound change. Groups such as the utopian socialist communities of the first half of the nineteenth century (Oneida, New Harmony, or Brook Farm), Socialists (such as Henry George, Edward Bellamy, Eugene Debs, John Dewey, Erich Fromm, and Rinehold Niebuhr), American Communists, followers of Marcus Garvey, contemporary black economic nationalists and some New Left writers have demanded major social change through fundamental restructuring of the economic and political systems. All those influenced by Marxist analysis have attacked the dominant values as a mere superstructure developed to protect vested economic interests. Despite their protests, the underlying attitudes and values expressed through American public policy toward the poor have shown marked similarities over 300 years. To understand their tenacity, it is necessary to consider the nature of the socialization process, and the high level of complacency about these values in American society.

Personal identity is formed by social processes, and once crystallized it is maintained, modified and even reshaped by social relations.[1] Thus, an individual born in the United States gains a particular sense of identity and view of reality which differs markedly from that of an individual born in another land. This view is transmitted by his primary contacts with family and peers who themselves have undergone the socialization process, and through contacts with social institutions (religious, educational or legal) whose functions are to conserve and transmit the socially accepted values. Thus, men both create the values and institutions of their society, and are created by them. Consequently, basic changes in the socialization process tend to occur slowly. Moreover, several factors support American values and help to explain the level of complacency that Americans feel about them. Among these are the relatively high standard of living enjoyed by the majority, the rapid growth during this century of a new middle class (which reinforces a belief in increased chances for occupational mobility), and a great expansion of educational opportunities (which offers hope for self-improvement). There has also been a slow drift toward income equalization among the employed if consideration is given to the benefits, such as pensions, hospital and medical aid which are available in most businesses. Naturally, the poor do not benefit, but this fact is conveniently overlooked by those who do.

Given the inherent conservatism of institutions of socialization, the pervasive commitment to materialistic individualism and racism and the level of complacency about values, the prospects for fundamental restructuring seem limited in the politically significant future, short of violent revolution. However, with the high level of support for American values and institutions which public opinion polls constantly bring out, success for a revolution is unlikely. The type of incremental change that does seem likely will apear trivial to American socialists.

In contrast, since organic liberals define poverty more simply as a question of minimum subsistence, they would welcome just such incremental change, and could be its architects. While "conservatives" often have sufficient power to block "liberal" initiatives, they are not strong enough to initiate by themselves. Consequently, the programs that organic liberals find acceptable appear to have the greatest chances of enactment during the next decade.

Many individuals and groups are concerned with specific programs to alleviate one particular aspect of poverty, such as child care centers, extension of public health services, or the like. But nibbling at the edges of the problem always has been the traditional method of dealing with poverty, which has produced the present inadequate and contradictory public policy. Rather, despite the difficulties in such analysis, it would seem most appropriate to consider the broader question of: How is it possible, without major institutional and social restructuring, to reduce poverty in America? The traditional liberal response since the New Deal era has been increasing dependence on a combination of the President who has the broadest, most representative constituency in the nation, plus a professionalized bureaucracy functionally integrating all public administration. The New Left has countered this with a demand for decentralization of policy formation which would involve the poor in planning the programs that affect their lives.

In assessing the value of these programs and attempting to draw conclusions regarding the most effective strategies for change, the author has no *sufficient* solutions to propose, but is attracted to several strategies because of their greater potential for reducing poverty. While they may appear modest for their lack of major rapid change, these suggestions are being presented *only* because more sweeping change is not currently possible. It seems more useful, then, to find a means to create conditions which could *expand* those limitations to allow wider possibilities on which the poor might capitalize. Those who may find such limited suggestions "unimpressive" might recall that it was considered a sufficiently difficult labor for Hercules to clean out the Augean stables. He was not then required to refill them.

INADEQUACY OF GREATER CENTRALIZATION

In dealing with questions of poverty, several writers maintain that the only protection for unorganized groups against organized elites can be found by strengthening the national government, especially the presidency. It is assumed that because the president alone has a national constituency, he can protect all of the unorganized against aggregations of power in organized elites.[2] Some critics go so far as to suggest that all governmental policies should be nationalized, that legislative authority should be coalesced with executive authority and that all public administration be functionally integrated.[3]

Further functional integration of public policy is quite likely in the future but hardly desirable for those who would escape the problems of elitism. Stripped of its humanist rhetoric, this is simply a 20th-century resurrection of Plato's Philosopher King and the Guardians, with all the problems inherent in that theory. As has been previously indicated, the implications of the trend toward professionalization in the administration of public policy are obvious: the greater the degree of functional integration, the harder it will be for the unorganized to be heard over the claims of large, effective economic lobbies.

The claim that a president with greater power would be able to control this process is hopelessly unrealistic. At present, there are about 9,517,000 civilian employees administering domestic policy in national, state and local governments in America.[4] This leaves 899,000 administering national domestic policy, 2,211,000 administering state policy and 6,407,000 administering local policy. And employment growth in state and especially local governments is rapidly accelerating. Consequently, even if Plato's Philosopher King could gain presidential office, his prospects seem dim for coordinating and enforcing responsibility to the public interest of ten to twelve million bureaucrats. Moreover, should such a paragon exist, the process through which American presidents are recruited could not be counted upon to include him.[5] Furthermore, the president has too many other demands on his time to attempt effective administration of domestic programs, even if it were possible. Given all the other tasks he must perform, domestic administration (particularly poverty programs) must have a relatively low priority for any president.

Without strong coordination from the Chief Executive, bureaucrats find it necessary to work out accords with the attentive pressure groups in their areas.[6] Thus, the demand for greater power in the presidency or more professionalized administration (however unintentional) is a demand for greater elitism.

This potential for even greater elitism raises a difficult question concerning the nature of elite rule in America: with whom must bureaucrats work out accords, who actually rules? In categorizing the nature of elite rule there is an inherent problem of distortion. The fewer the categories the more simplistic (therefore distorted) the analysis. C. Wright Mills was the most conspicious of the writers whose model of the nature of elite rule in America was badly oversimplified.[7] In *The Power Elite* he claimed that a military-industrial complex ran America. All policy was viewed as a reflection of the conscious planning and desires of that elite. If his analysis were true, only violent revolution could change the situation, which would be a counsel of despair to the poor because such revolution seems improbable.

Fortunately for those who desire change, it is a false picture. Since a variety of analysts have detailed the ways in which Mills' military-industrial complex is unrealistic, here are a few major arguments:

1. *M.I.C. lacks sufficient unity:* The industrial or corporate elite is not monolithic, even on policies directly related to corporate desires.

For example, when the automotive industry wants low tariffs on imported steel so that it can buy cheaply, the steel industry wants high tariffs so that it can sell steel at high prices. Furthermore, corporations are staffed by professional administrators ("managerial elite") who have their own self-interest, which includes a greater acceptance of the values of the prevailing liberal concensus than was shared by industrialists of the past.[8]

2. *M.I.C. lacks sufficient rationality:* Like the "masses," the corporate and military elites may have "false consciousness." As one analyst noted, they do not always take a position in accord with their rational interests. Instead, they can sometimes be self-deluded, or deluded by other elites, especially the political elite or various professional elites.[9]

3. *Political actors are not simple rubber stamps for military-industrial goals:* The political elite is hardly monolithic.[10] For example, the legislative elite and the executive differ profoundly on many issues. Substantial differences occur between local, state and national governments. Professional administrators with their own self-interests are not found solely in the corporate, financial and industrial world ("managerial elite"): The federal government employs two and a half million civilians in its vast bureaucracy, and no recent president would claim that they followed his directives. The extent of this decentralization makes it possible for individuals and groups which do organize, to successfully oppose the initiatives of the "military-industrial complex" on many occasions. For example, the Mills argument simply cannot account for the defeat of the S.S.T., the impact of Ralph Nader, the effect of the ecology movement of the early 1970s, or the fact that military appropriations and troop strength have frequently been cut in a manner which has run directly counter to the desires of the military and many sectors of industry.

4. *M.I.C. lacks sufficient breadth of interest:* The primary domain of the "military-industrial complex" is defense and foreign policy. It is not interested in most domestic questions. If one analyzes the manner in which public policy on education, the distribution of medical services, welfare, sanitation, recreation, or myriad other domestic programs is formulated, one finds that there are *many* elites in America each of whom has *specialized* interests. Therefore, only a few may be involved in any given area. They tend to interlock only temporarily and for limited types of issues, with some issues being determined in a "democratic" fashion by the larger voting public on the occasions when it mobilizes itself with interest and action on those issues.[11]

5. *Mills ignores non-decision making:* As Robert Wolff suggested, the fact that the policies of its rulers are wrong is not by itself evidence of the existence of a power elite: "Those who rule in this country do so by default. . . . The most significant fact about the distribution of power in America is not who makes such decisions as are made, but rather, how many matters of the greatest social importance are not objects of anyone's decision at all."[12]

In short, no single elite rules America. Instead, public policy is formulated by multiple specialized elites. The reason corporate and military interests are so often the basis of public policy is due to the fact that these interests accord with the dominant, pervasive values which a majority of Americans accept—materialistic individualism and ethnocentrism.[13] In allocating resources most Americans have accepted the primacy of their needs. However, that frequently reflects "false consciousness" in the sense that majority interests often are not served by what is "best for General Motors," as in the need to force automotive manufacturers to install safety devices, or the need for other forms of consumer protection.

The significance of this analysis for those who wish to reduce poverty is twofold. First, the more centralized and functionally oriented the formulation and administration of public policy, the less likely it is that the needs or interests of the poor will be considered. Consequently, the functional orientation of the civil service must be checked. Second, the fact that public policy is formulated by specialized elites means that those who wish to reduce poverty do not have to fight the entire "military-industrial complex." Naturally, decisions about the allocation of resources in which corporate interests are involved can have serious consequences for poverty policy. (For example, without substantially increased taxes, it was not possible to wage both the Vietnamese War and the War on Poverty.) Nevertheless, decisions can still be made about the use to which the remaining resources are put. In addition, with organization and persistent effort it may be possible to raise the level of consciousness of other groups to the fact that resources are maldistributed since they, too, are adversely affected, as well as the poor. This requires greater decentralization.

While there are many means which can be devised to limit the functional orientation of the bureaucracy, there is a case in point. At present, most civil service regulations for localities, states and the national government require narrow specialization for promotion. Men rise through the ranks in a particular agency and their years of specialization in that institution plus their job tenure enables them to develop a specialized perspective oriented toward self-perpetuation rather than performance. Some useful reform might include opening entry to an agency in different governments (local, state and national), not just to one,[14] allowing personnel to move freely between different agencies in the same goverment and regulation of the length of time an individual could spend in one agency. Similarly, the Intergovernmental Personnel Act of 1968 was a useful step in enabling men to move between local, state and national governments without loss of tenure or pension rights. This allows more interchange in the system, less fixed professional interests and more performance orientation.

DECENTRALIZATION

The degree to which such change will be useful to the needs of the poor will depend upon the degree to which it is possible to attain more fundamental restructuring of the pressures on government through decentralization, which could provide the impetus for many further reforms. Neither will it be easy nor a complete panacea, but it appears to be a fruitful means for laying the groundwork for greater change.

Fundamentally, we do not need new agencies, but we do need new ways to control those that we already have. To enable greater community participation, decentralization is an important tool because of its potential for: 1) changing the destructive self-image of the poor; 2) coopting others;[15] 3) effecting substantive policy change; and 4) providing legitimacy for public policy.

Since the poor's negative self-image has tended to hinder them from developing alternative policies, greater community participation would have the potential for building self-confidence and a sense of identity by overcoming the alienation, apathy and despair that has been so destructive.[16] The poor do have expertise in that they are aware of some problems which institutions should be solving and are qualified to judge how effectively their goals are being accomplished.[17] This is the "consumer perspective, the perspective of the persons who must live day to day with the end results of those efforts."[18] Their expertise, then, gives them potential for developing alternative policies to those currently being applied. If a means is provided, such as decentralization, they can grow and develop in the process. The impact of the various power movements of the 60s and 70s (black, brown, red and gold) on their members' self-confidence and political effectiveness illustrates the point. These movements began to destroy previous apathy as blacks, Mexican-Americans, Puerto Ricans, Indians and Chinese-Americans discovered that it was possible for them to have some influence on the system. Organization spread and developed, helping to change their destructive self-image to one of power and consequence.

A second asset of decentralization is the potential for winning allies. The powerless may activate other groups to fight on their behalf.[19] As Kenneth Clark has indicated, the poor are not equipped to engage sophisticated adversaries, therefore, they need to work out a coalition with professionals.[20] Studies have revealed that leaders are more predisposed to support liberal values than are masses in America.[21] This is particularly true of the upper echelons of the highly influential communications, publishing and academic elites. To the degree that they live in ignorance of a problem, they will not act. Therefore, it is necessary for disadvantaged groups to organize and find effective means to capture their attention.

The black movement was quite effective in this regard, thereby significantly altering the quantity and substance of information about blacks which was disseminated through the mass media, publishing, and the educational system. Furthermore, not all professionals in education, medicine, law, social or welfare work and the government share the prevailing norms of their professions. Moreover, black organization caused many previous opponents to retreat or to become ambivalent.[22] In addition, organizations informed the bureaucracy and monitored its activities, thereby increasing the visibility of the decision-making process and causing it to represent a set of interests which previously had been ignored.[23] Miller and Riessman argue that community organization can move the political center of gravity further toward the interests for which they had organized, thereby providing more leverage with traditional agencies and power structures.[24]

The pay-off in public policy may be seen in the example of the black movement. While policy development was halting and inadequate, blacks did cause some significant changes in the manner in which they were treated by groups, such as the media, universities, welfare agencies, corporate employment officers, labor unions, voting registrars, and the United States Army. The impact of these changes on American values will be increasingly felt in succeeding decades. Already, studies reveal that young whites are less racist than their parents, having been exposed to different images.[25] (These studies indicate that this is a difference between generations, not a consequence of youth that will change with age.) If the poor can organize more effectively, they may undergo a similar development with attendant impact on relevant American values.

In short, if the decision-making centers are restructured so that it is possible for people in all walks of life to participate in decisions that affect them, those unorganized groups which have been disadvantaged by the present system could benefit in substantive policy terms[26]—another potential asset of community participation.

An example of the value of geographic decentralized decision-making centers may be taken from the New York City public school system, in which a majority of the students (50.2%) are black and Puerto Rican,[27] primarily from working class or poor backgrounds but whose teachers are overwhelmingly middle-class whites from different ethnic and cultural backgrounds, who frequently appear to despise their students' traditions.[28]

The attendant impact on black and Puerto Rican students is partially reflected in their extraordinarily high dropout rate. While they comprise 38 percent of the students in all New York City academic high schools (the system also has commercial and vocational high schools, and special high schools for problem children), it is estimated that they receive only 5.3% of all academic diplomas awarded annually. If the autonomy of the educational elite were ended by administering policy on a dispersed geographic basis (decentralizing the school system) those affected by its policies could have some voice in determining them. A similar effect would occur in *all* areas of public policy if the functional orientation of those who administer policy were subordinated to a geographic one.

Many critics argue that the *form* of community control in education may be appealing, but no *substantial* policy difference will occur.[29] To this objection two brief responses seem appropriate. First, there *is* some difference in substance as indicated by the experience of New York City's recent demonstration school districts.[30] Second, as Charles Hamilton pointed out, the question of community control is related to more than a simple question of the performance of public institutions. It relates to their *legitimacy* as well.[31] Institutions in a democracy cannot be said to formulate public policy in a legitimate manner if they exclude from consideration the concerns and needs of those who are affected by their policies.

These assets are significant, but they are only potentials. Several problems must be overcome before community participation can achieve its objectives. A crucial one is the difficulty of organizing the poor to take advantage of their options, because they would not automatically have a large voice in a decentralized system unless they *were* organized.[32] As has been suggested, they are a diverse group, lacking a common sense of identity, and suffering from several mutual antagonisms. Moreover, *sustained* initiative is necessary, which is particularly difficult for the poor.[33] However, recent experience with the Community Action Program indicates that the *most effective* way to organize the poor is around immediate, concrete community development and social action objectives.[34] To say that organization is difficult is not to eliminate it as a possibility. Essentially, there is more likelihood of successful, sustained organization if policy making is decentralized than in a functionally integrated system.

Another problem is the lack of financial resources available to the poor, since decentralization cannot be effective unless resources remain available for poor neighborhoods. If community participation remains merely a matter of power rhetoric, it is likely to backfire by creating greater frustration and alienation among the disillusioned.[35] There has been an increase in just such attitudes during this decade, as demonstrated by increasing violence and riots. Particularly among nonwhites, there has been a growing demand for withdrawal from American society. In 1969, for example, a Gallup poll found that one fifth of all American blacks desired a separate nation within the United States.[36] Indicative of future levels of alienation and despair, unless major changes occur, was the fact that one quarter of those under thirty desired a separate nation.[37] Similar separatist demands have been voiced by some Indian groups, and some Mexican-Americans in the Southwest.

At least some degree of frustration is inevitable for any group, because a pluralistic society cannot fully satisfy any one interest; but it seems probable that the greater resources of other groups will always provide them with advantages over the poor in attaining their ends. Therefore, the poor are bound to face numerous obstacles in developing effective organization.

Nevertheless, even though organization of the poor may begin in a small and relatively disjointed manner, it has the potential for laying the groundwork for more fundamental change, as may be seen by the progress of several types of community organization and influence throughout the last decade. To illustrate, Mexican-American organization of farm workers under Cesar Chavez finally won a settlement of the five-year-old grape picker's strike, which symbolized the growing militancy and organization of Mexican-Americans in rural and urban-areas throughout the nation.[38] *La Raza Unida* (The United People) has recently played a militant role in Texas politics as both a brown power movement and a political party, and already has made some gains in achieving its demands.[39] In the *barrio* of East Los Angeles, in Denver, in New Mexico, and throughout the Southwest, organization is beginnning and is aiming at specific community goals.[40] Communities as far north as Oregon and Idaho are feeling the impact of similar organization.[41]

Black civil rights and community organizations are better known, and have achieved some goals, such as community schools, hospitals, welfare regulations, and have elected some representatives to local, state and national offices. This is reflected in a recent study which attributed the lessening "expressive disorders" (riots) in black urban ghettos to an increased involvement by the community and its leaders in issue-oriented politics.[42] At the end of the 1960s, Indians were also beginning to organize in the Southwest[43] as were Chinese in both San Francisco and New York City, and Puerto Ricans in New York City.

These suggestions for checks on the functional orientation of the civil service and decentralization will not "solve" the problems of the poor, but they are indicative of useful areas of experimentation. Any demand for a thorough-going solution is presently unrealistic and self-defeating in America. Given the widespread public attitudes toward the poor in general, and those racial and ethnic minorities disproportionately represented among the poor in particular, change in the direction of greater democracy would seem to provide the best opportunity *currently* available for reform. It at least holds the potential of laying the groundwork for more fundamental reform in the future.

The problems of the poor in America and the possibility for change are combined in a paraphrase of St. Matthew: Unto everyone that hath the means to affect public policy "shall be given, and he shall have abundance; but from him that hath not shall be taken away even that which he hath."[44]

Notes

1. PETER L. BERGER and THOMAS LUCKMANN, *The Social Construction of Reality* (Garden City, N. Y.: Doubleday, 1966), p. 173.

2. GRANT MCCONNELL, *Private Power and American Democracy* (New York: Alfred A. Knopf, 1967).

3. HENRY S. KARIEL, *The Decline of American Pluralism* (Stanford, Calif.: Stanford University Press, 1961).

4. *The Book of the States 1968–1969*, The Council of State Governments, Chicago (1968), p. 163.

5. D. JAMES, *The Contemporary Presidency*, chap. 1.

6. This process was described for those regulatory commissions that have been established independent of the president in MARVER BERNSTEIN, *Regulating Business by Independent Commission* (Princeton, N. J.: Princeton University Press, 1955).

7. C. WRIGHT MILLS, *The Power Elite* (New York: Oxford University Press, 1956).

8. A. A. BERLE, *Power Without Property* (New York: Harcourt Brace Jovanovich, Inc., 1959), pp. 90–91.

9. ARNOLD M. ROSE, *The Power Structure* (New York: Oxford University Press, 1967).

10. THOMAS R. DYE and L. HARMON ZEIGLER, *The Irony of Democracy* (Belmont, Calif.: Wadsworth Publishing, 1970), chap. 4.

11. ROSE, *The Power Structure*.

12. ROBERT WOLFF, *The Poverty of Liberalism*, pp. 117–118.

13. For a similar analysis using somewhat different terms, see GABRIEL KOLKO, *The Roots of American Foreign Policy* (Boston: Beacon Press, 1969), chap. 1. He views the corporate structure as determining American values. I believe that the process demonstrates more interaction. For reasons discussed in chap. 2, Americans valued materialistic individualism and ethnocentrism. Therefore, the corporate community found ready acceptance for its views, and further contributed to reinforcing American beliefs in these values.

14. PAUL T. DAVID and ROSS POLLOCK, *Executives for Government* (Washington, D.C.: Brookings Institution, 1957), pp. 63–66.

15. PETER BACHRACH and MORTON S. BARATZ, *Power and Poverty* (New York: Oxford University Press, 1970), pp. 201–213.

16. ALAN A. ALTSHULER, *Community Control* (New York: Pegasus, 1970), p. 210.

17. STEVEN A. WALDHORN, "Legal Intervention and Citizen Participation as Strategies for Change in Public-Serving Bureaucracies," paper prepared for the annual meeting of the American Political Science Association, New York City (September 4, 1969), p. 23.

18. JEAN and EDGAR CAHN, "Citizen Participation," *Citizen Participation in Urban Development*, HANS SPIEGEL, ed., vol. 1 (Washington, D. C.: NTL Institute for Applied Behavioral Science, 1968), p. 220.

19. MICHAEL LIPSKY, *Protest in City Politics* (Chicago: Rand McNally, 1970), p. 201.

20. KENNETH B. CLARK and JEANETTE HOPKINS, *A Relevant War Against Poverty* (New York: Harper & Row, 1969), p. 254.

21. SAMUEL S. STOUFFER, *Communism, Conformity, and Civil Liberties* (New York: Doubleday, 1955).

22. WARREN C. HAGGSTROM, "Can the Poor Transform the World?", *Readings in Community Organization Practice*, RALPH M. KRAMER and HARRY SPECHT, eds. (Englewood Cliffs, N. J.: Prentice-Hall, 1969), p. 303.

23. WALDHORN, "Legal Intervention and Citizen Participation As Strategies for Change in Public-Serving Bureaucracies," pp. 24-25.

24. MILLER & RIESSMAN, *Social Class and Social Policy*, p. 231.

25. See FRED I. GREENSTEIN, *Children and Politics* (New Haven, Conn.: Yale University Press, 1965); and ROBINSON, RUSK & HEAD, *Measures of Political Attitudes*.

26. PETER BACHRACH, *The Theory of Democratic Elitism* (Boston: Little, Brown, 1967).

27. All figures on New York City pupils from the Master Plan of the Board of Higher Education for the City University of New York, 1968.

28. H.A.R.Y.O.U.; EDDY, *Walk the White Line*; MARILYN GITTELL and ALAN HEVESI, eds., *The Politics of Urban Education* (New York: Frederick Praeger, 1969); DAVID ROGERS, *110 Livingston Street* (New York: Vintage, 1969); MARILYN GITTELL, *Participants and Participation* (New York: Praeger, 1968).

29. EDWARD C. BANFIELD, *The Unheavenly City* (Boston: Little, Brown, 1970); DANIEL P. MOYNIHAN, "Policy vs. Program in the 70's," *The Public Interest* (Summer 1970), 90–100; JAMES Q. WILSON, "The Urban Unease," *The Public Interest* (Summer 1968), 26–27.

30. For several articles on the New York experience as well as that of other cities see GITTELL and HEVESI, eds., *The Politics of Urban Education.*

31. CHARLES V. HAMILTON, "Conflict, Race and System Transformation," *Journal of International Affairs*, 23 (1969), 106–118.

32. For analysis of underlying problems see MICHAEL LIPSKY, "Protest As a Political Resource," *The American Political Science Review*, 62 (December 1968), 1144–1158.

33. PETER MARRIS and MARTIN REIN, *Dilemmas of Social Reform* (New York: Atherton Press, 1967), p. 231.

34. KRAMER, *Participation of the Poor*, p. 270.

35. LIPSKY, "Protest As a Political Resource," pp. 1157–1158; CLARK & HOPKINS, *A Relevant War Against Poverty*, pp. 248–249.

36. *Newsweek*, 73 (June 30, 1969), 19.

37. *Ibid.*, p. 21.

38. S. STEINER, *Mexicans*; PETER MATTHEISSEN, *Sal Si Puedes* (New York: Random House, 1970); EUGENE NELSON, *Huelga: The First Hundred Days of the Great Delano Grape Strike* (Delano, Calif.: Farm Workers Press, 1966).

39. *The New York Times*, August 2, 1970, 1:5.

40. *The New York Times*, April 20, 1969, 1:7.

41. *The Intermountain Observer* of Boise, Idaho, November 21, 1970, 6:1.

42. MARIAN LIEF PALLEY and HOWARD A. PALLEY, "From Expressive Disorders to Issue-Oriented Politics," paper prepared for the sixty-sixth Annual Meeting of the American Political Science Association, Los Angeles, Calif. (September 8–12, 1970).

43. *The New York Times*, October 12, 1969, 86:4; *The New York Times*, December 7, 1969, 81:1; VINE DELORIA, "The War Between the Redskins and the Feds," *The New York Times Magazine* (December 7, 1969), pp. 47–102.

44. MATTHEW, XXV, 21.

Index